JOHN WESLEY AND HIS DOCTRINE

William McDonald

Author of

Modern Faith Healing Scripturally Considered

Satan and Annihiliation

(with E.M. Bounds)

SCHMUL PUBLISHING COMPANY
NICHOLASVILLE, KENTUCKY

This Schmul Publishing Co. edition is not a scanned facsimile of a used book. It has not been "updated" or edited into modern English, punctuation or grammar, but is accurate to the author's own style and usage. The text has been carefully proofread for accuracy and formatted for easier reading by today's readers. Every effort has been made to prevent disordered text.

Published by Schmul Publishing Co.
PO Box 776
Nicholasville, KY 40340
USA

Printed in the United States of America

ISBN 10: 0-88019-639-4
ISBN 13: 978-0-88019-639-0

Visit us on the Internet at www.wesleyanbooks.com, or order direct from the publisher by calling 800-772-6657, or by writing to the above address.

Contents

Publisher's Preface

William McDonald was born in Belmont, Maine, on March 1, 1820. And on March 20, 1838, he was born again, in a Belfast Methodist class meeting. He joined the Methodist Episcopal Church at the Maine Annual Conference of 1840 and accepted the responsibility for a circuit consisting of six preaching points, to which he walked. He quickly rose in abilities and prominence until by the time he was only twenty-nine he was pastor of the largest and most important Methodist church in the state.

At Kennebunk Camp Meeting in Maine, on August 16, 1857, he received the Second Blessing of Entire Sanctification.

Almost immediately he received a divine call to enter the field of evangelism, over which he struggled for several years. He declined to be an evangelist, spent several years in financial reverses and lost the inner witness to his experience. He would later admit that this time had caused both his ministerial and spiritual life to suffer.

In 1868, McDonald became active in the National Camp Meeting Association for the Promotion of Holiness and was elected its vice-president. Tightening those bonds in July 1870, McDonald became the founding editor of the *Advocate of Christian Holiness*, the publication of the Association.

At last, in 1871 he announced he was responding to the call to be an evangelist with John S. Inskip, the first president of the Association. The two complemented each other— Inskip as a fiery preacher, McDonald as a calm, measured teacher of holiness. Both were convinced that the Methodist doctrine of holiness must be the centerpiece of their revival efforts. Together they witnessed thousands of souls saved and sanctified in their evangelistic travels around the world.

After the death of John Inskip, McDonald was elected president of the National Campmeeting Association at the age of sixty-four. For the next ten years he led the group ably, expanding the membership to include many more ministers from the North and East, and numbered on its rolls representatives from the West and the South as well. He made multiple trips to the West, holding revivals, and was instrumental in leading the pastor of Los Angeles First Methodist Church, Phineas F. Bresee, into the Second Blessing. Bresee would later go on to found the Church of the Nazarene.

During the late 1800s, however, the doctrine of Christian perfection as taught by John Wesley was increasingly challenged, paralleled by rising worldly accommodation in the church. Wesley's fear that growing materialism would undo his beloved Methodists was coming to pass. Like their founder, holiness advocates found themselves ostracized and ridiculed.

McDonald urged people to remain as holiness missionaries within the Methodist Episcopal Church. Regardless of his best efforts, though, many left or were thrust out by anti-holiness congregations, ministers and bishops. He remonstrated against the move but could not stem the rising tide of "come-out-ism" as holiness people left to form new holiness churches.

It was during this dark time he felt the need to address false claims by the opponents of Christian perfection—assertions that Wesley himself did not advocate it as a second work of grace, or if he had, he changed his mind in his later years. This small, easy-to-read volume, *John Wesley and His Doctrine,* ably rose to the challenge.

Today, scholars and preachers in many of those same groups now repeat the errors of the late nineteenth century, casting aspersion on the doctrine, doubting its historical veracity, and looking askance at those who still hold to it. In such an environment, McDonald's work rises again to affirm the solid truths of scriptural holiness as proclaimed by John Wesley and the early Methodists.

William McDonald, evangelist, pastor, songwriter, publisher, editor and author, retired in 1894, and died on September 11, 1901, in Somerville, Massachusetts, faithful to the last.

—D. Curtis Hale
Publisher, 2021

Preface

It was not our purpose in preparing the first part of this volume to furnish a complete life of John Wesley. Our object was to present, in a plain, brief, comprehensive form, enough of that remarkable life to give the common reader a clear understanding of *who* he was, and *what* he did. To this end, we have sketched, briefly, the incidents of his early history; of his toils and hardships in America; of his marked religious experience; of his unexampled labors; of his unparalleled persecutions, with the victories and triumphs which crowned his remarkable career. We have retained all that is essential to be known of the life and labors of this great and good man, and have presented it in a form to be quickly read and easily understood. It will have less interest for the Church historian, than for those who have little time for reading larger and more expensive volumes.

The *second part* of this volume is devoted to a comprehensive presentation of the doctrine of *Christian perfection,*— the "central idea" in Mr. Wesley's system of evangelical truth.

We have sought to present this doctrine in its various aspects, mainly in the language of Mr. Wesley himself.

We have attempted an answer to a variety of objections to the Wesleyan view of heart purity, as a second, distinct work, and with how much success, we leave the reader to judge. We think we have demonstrated, beyond successful contradiction, that Mr. Wesley, from 1770 to the end of life, never changed his views on this subject in one essential point, much less did he ever "cancel" his lifelong doctrine of "Sin in Believers."

Our greatest desire is that our readers may know the actual experience of heart purity, so clearly taught in this volume. This will settle every doubt.

BOSTON, June 1, 1893. W. MCDONALD

Chapter I.
Born in Troublous Times.

During the latter part of the seventeenth and the first part of the eighteenth century, England was the theater of stirring events. War sounded its clarion notes through the land. Marlborough had achieved a series of brilliant victories on the continent, which had filled and fired the nation's heart with the spirit of military glory.

The English, at this time, had an instinctive horror of popery and power. They had hurled the king, James II., from the throne, because he was a papist and a tyrant, and now his grandson, Charles Edward, known as the Pretender, was making every possible effort to regain the throne, and to subject the people to absolute despotism. To add to their dismay, the fleets of France and Spain were hovering along the English coast, ready at any favorable moment to pounce upon her. The means of public communication by railroad and telegraph were unknown. There were few mails, and consequently reliable information could not be readily or safely obtained. Under such circumstances it is not surprising that strange and exaggerated reports should have kept the public mind in a state of great excitement and general consternation.

It was pre-eminently an infidel age. Disrespect for the Bible and the Christian religion prevailed among all classes. Hobbes, with his scorpion tongue; Toland, with his papal-poisoned heart; Tindal, with an infidel dagger concealed under a cloak of mingled popery and Protestantism; Collins, with a heart full of hatred for the Christian religion; Chubb, with his deistical insidiousness; and Shaftesbury, with his platonic skepticism, hurled by wit and sarcasm,— these, with their corrupt associates, made that the infidel age of the world. Christianity was everywhere held up to public reprobation and scorn.

It is said to have been also the Augustine age of English literature. The wonderful discoveries of Newton had filled the civilized world with amazement. The brilliant productions of Addison, Steele, Swift, Pope and others had, in too many instances, been substituted for the Word of God, and great numbers sold their heavenly birthright for less than a mess of pottage.

Added to this, the Church, which should have been the light of the world, was in a most deplorable state. Irreligion and spiritual indifference had taken possession of priest and people, and ministers were sleeping over the threatened ruin of the church, and in too many instances were hastening, by their open infidelity, the day of her ruin.

The Established Church overtopped everything. She possessed great power and little piety. Her sacerdotal robes had displaced the garments of holiness; her prayer book had well-nigh extinguished those earnest soul-breathings which bring the heart into union with the Crucified. Spirituality had almost found a grave, from which it was feared there would be no resurrection.

Over this sad state of things a few were found who made bitter lamentations. Bishop Burnett was "filled with sad thoughts." Bishop Gibson gives a heart-saddening picture of the times. Bishop Butter declares the church to be only a subject of mirth and ridicule. Guyse says, "that preachers and people were content to lay Christ aside." Hurrion sees "faith, joy and Christian zeal under a thick cloud." Taylor declares "that the Spirit was grieved and offended by the abominable corruptions that abound;" while good old Dr. Watts sings sadly of the "poor dying rate" at which the professed friends of Jesus lived.

This was the state of England when, June 17th, 1703, was born at Epworth, of Samuel and Susannah Wesley, the subject of this writing—John Wesley.

Samuel Wesley, father of John, was for some forty years rector of Epworth Parish. He was an honest, conscientious, stern old Englishman—a firmer never clung to the mane of the British lion. He was always poor, but always honest. He was often in jail for debt, and as often relieved by donations from the Duke of Buckingham, the Archbishop of York, the Queen and others. "No man," he says, "has worked truer for bread than I have done, and no man has lived harder."

He was no conservative in politics. He espoused most heartily the cause of William, Prince of Orange, regarding him as a perfect antitype of Job's war horse, and received in return for such support the anathemas of his parishioners. They stabbed his cow, cut off his dog's legs, burned his flax and twice fired his house. Tyerman says he was "learned, laborious and godly." He had the reputation of being a good poet, a fair commentator and a respectable miscellaneous writer.

Susannah Wesley was the perfect antipodes of her husband. She was beautiful, amiable, thoughtful, devout, energetic and intelligent. She had mastered Greek, Latin and French, and was the mother of nineteen children. Of her, Dr. Adam Clarke says, "Such a woman, take her for all in all, I have not read of, nor with her equal have I been acquainted. Many daughters have done virtuously, but Susannah Wesley has excelled them all."

She was the sole instructress of her numerous family—and "such a family," continues Dr. Clarke, "I have never read of, heard of, or known; nor since the days of Abraham and Sarah, Joseph and Mary, of Nazareth, has there been a family to which the human race has been more indebted." Had not Susannah Wesley been the mother of John Wesley, it is not likely that John Wesley would have been the founder of Methodism.

His early life.

During the first eleven years of Mr. Wesley's life little worthy of note occurred, except that he was rescued, at the age of five, from the burning parsonage, almost by miracle; his father believing from that time that God designed him for some special work, and a similar impression following the youth as well.

Wesley's education, during his early years, devolved principally upon his mother. His sobriety was so marked, his conduct so consistent, and his whole life so faultless, that at the age of eight years his father admitted him to the sacrament.

Passing from the watchful eye of his father, and the tender, loving and almost unexampled care and the instruction of his mother, he entered, at the age of eleven, or possibly a little earlier, what is known as the Charter House School, London. In this he was largely aided by the Duke of Buckingham, who seems to have been a fast friend of his father. Here he remained some six years, distinguishing himself in every branch of scholarship to which he turned his attention. Being a charity scholar, however, he did not escape the taunts of fellow-students more highly favored than he; but he bore all these with meekness, patiently suffering wrongfully.

Mr. Tyerman, who seems to have searched for every

spot on this rising sun, is bold to say that Wesley "lost the religion which had marked his character from the days of his infancy. He entered the Charter House a saint, and left it a sinner." We cannot find this marked change on the record, with the clearness with which it appears to Mr. Tyerman. There is no evidence that Wesley had ever known the converting grace of God up to this time, and if not, we are unable to see how he could have lost it. That he was a sinner at this time there can be no doubt. But while he confesses that he was a sinner, he declares that his "sins were not scandalous in the eyes of the world." Instead of being the wicked boy that Mr. Tyerman represents him to have been, he declares, "I still read the Scriptures, and said my prayers morning and evening. And what I now hoped to be saved by was: 1. Not being as bad as other people. 2. Having still a kindness for religion; and 3. Reading my Bible, going to church, and saying my prayers."

Should a young man, in these times, in passing through Harvard, Princeton or Middletown, give evidence that he read his Bible, prayed morning and evening, attended church regularly, joined in all the devotions, went to the sacrament, and manifested a kindness for religion, who would say that "He entered college a saint and left it a sinner?" There is no evidence that Wesley, during his six years' course at the Charter House, ever contracted vicious habits, or became a flagrant sinner. The wonder is that, with such corrupt and corrupting influences surrounding him, he had not been morally ruined.

At the age of seventeen he entered Christ College, Oxford. Here he remained some four years, distinguishing himself as an acute logician, fine classical scholar, and acquiring some knowledge of Hebrew. His means of support were limited, requiring the greatest economy, which he studiously practiced.

At the age of twenty-one, while yet a student at Oxford, "he appeared," says a writer of the times, "the very sensible and acute collegian; a young fellow of the finest classical taste, of the most liberal and manly sentiments." In September of this year, 1725, he was ordained deacon by Bishop Potter, and in March, of the following year was elected Fellow of Lincoln College.

In his new and elevated position, he devoted himself to the study of the Greek and Roman historians and poets, to logic, ethics, natural philosophy, oratory, Hebrew and Arabic. He perfected himself in French, and both spoke and wrote Latin with remarkable purity and correctness. He gave also considerable attention to the study of medicine.

It was while he was a member of Lincoln College that that unparalleled religious career of Mr. Wesley, which has always been regarded as the most wonderful religious movement of modern times, began. "Whoever studies the simplicity of its beginning, the rapidity of its growth, the stability of its institutions, its present vitality and activity, its commanding position and prospective greatness, must confess the work to be, not of man, but of God."

The heart of the youthful collegian was profoundly stirred by the reading of the "Christian Pattern" by Thomas á Kempis, and "Holy Living and Dying," by Jeremy Taylor. He learned from the former "that simplicity of intention and purity of affection were the wings of the soul, without which he could never ascend to God;" and on reading the latter he instantly resolved to dedicate all his life to God. He was convinced that there was no medium; every part must be a sacrifice to either God or himself. From this time his whole life was changed. How much he owed under God to these two works, eternity only will reveal. Law's "Call" and "Perfection" greatly aided him.

A little band was formed of such as professed to seek for all the mind of Christ. They commenced with four, but soon their number increased to six, then to eight, and so on. Their object was purely mutual profit. They read the classics on week days and divinity on the Sabbath. They prayed, fasted, visited the sick, the poor, the imprisoned. They were near to administer religious consolation to criminals in the hour of their execution. The names of these remarkable religious reformers were, John and Charles Wesley, Robert Kirkham, William Morgan, George Whitefield, John Clayton, J. Broughton, B. Ingham, J. Harvey, J. Whilelamb, W. Hall, J. Gambold, C. Kinchin, W. Smith, and Messrs. Salmon Morgan, Boyce and others.

As might have been expected, they were ridiculed and lampooned by those who differed from them, and who could not comprehend the motive to such a religions life. They were called, in derision, "Sacramentarians," "Bible Bigots," "Bible Moths," "The Holy Club," "The Godly Club," "Supererogation Men," and finally, "Methodists." Their strict, methodical lives, in the arrangement of their studies and the improvement of their time, their serious deportment and strict attention to religious duties, caused a jovial friend of Charles Wesley to say, "Why, here is a new sect of Methodists springing up," alluding to a school of ancient physicians, or to a class of nonconforming ministers of the seventeenth century, or to both, who received this title from some things common to both. The name took, and the young men were known throughout the university as the Methodists. The name, thus given in derision, was finally accepted, and has been retained in honor to this day.

A writer in one of the most respectable journals of the day, in describing these inoffensive men, employed the most unwarrantable language. It was affirmed that they had a near affinity to the Essenes among the Jews, and the Pietists of Switzerland; they excluded what was absolutely necessary to the support of life; they afflicted their bodies; they let blood once a fortnight, to keep down the carnal man; they allow none to have any religion but those of their own sect, while they themselves were farthest from it. They were hypocrites, and were supposed to use religion, only as a veil to vice; and their greatest friends were ashamed to stand in their defence. They were enthusiasts, madmen, fools and zealots. They pretend to be more pious than their neighbors. These were but the beginning of sorrows, as we shall see later.

In the midst of these scenes of persecution Wesley addressed a letter to his venerable father, still living at Epworth, asking his advice. The old man urged him to go on and not be weary in well-doing; "to bear no more sail than necessary, but to steer steady. As they had called his son the father of the Holy Club, they might call him the grandfather, and he would glory in that name, rather than in the title of *his Holiness."* These were noble words from sire to son at such a time and in such a conflict.

His father closing his earthly career about this time, John was urged to accept the Epworth living. But he could not conscientiously consent to do so but accepted a call from the governor of Georgia to come to America and preach the Gospel to the Indians.

In after years, when looking back upon the scenes of Oxford, and that mustard-seed beginning, Wesley says, "Two young men, without name, without friends, without either power or fortune, set out from college with principles totally different from those of the common people, to oppose all the world, learned and unlearned; and to combat popular prejudices of every kind. Their first principle directly attacked all wickedness; their second, all the bigotry in the world. Thus they attempted a reformation, not of opinions (feathers, trifles not worth naming) but of men's tempers and lives; of vice of every kind; of everything contrary to justice, mercy or truth. And for this it was, that they carried their lives in their hands, and that both the great, vulgar and the small looked upon them as mad dogs, and treated them as such." Such was the beginning of the religious career of this wonderful man.

Chapter II.
Wesley in America.

One of the most remarkable chapters in the life of John Wesley relates to his mission to America.

There was a tract of land in North America, lying between South Carolina and Florida, over which the English held a nominal jurisdiction. It was a wild, unexplored wilderness, inhabited only by Indian tribes. Under the sanction of a royal charter, in 1732, a settlement was made in this territory, and, as a compliment to the king, George II., it was named Georgia.

The object of such a settlement was twofold: first, to supply an outlet for the redundant population of the English metropolis; and secondly, to furnish a safe asylum for foreign Protestants who were the subjects of popish intolerance. No Roman Catholic could find a home there. James Edward Oglethorpe, an earnest friend of humanity, was appointed the first governor of the territory; and he, with twenty others, were named as trustees, to hold the territory twenty years in trust for the poor.

The first company of emigrants, one hundred and twenty-four in number, had already landed at Savannah, and were breathing its balmy air; and the enthusiastic governor was on his return, to inspire in the mind of the English people increased confidence in the new enterprise.

Having long been a personal friend of the Wesley family, Oglethorpe knew well the sterling worth of the two brothers—John and Charles—who were still at Oxford. An application was made to some of the Oxford Methodists to settle in the new colony as clergymen. Such sacrifices as they were ready to endure, and such a spirit as seemed to inflame them, were regarded as excellent qualities for the hardships of such a country as Georgia. Mr. Wesley was earnestly pressed by no less a person than the famous Dr. Burton, to undertake a mission to the Indians of Georgia, Dr. Burton telling him that "plausible and popular doctors of divinity were not the men wanted in Georgia," but men "inured to contempt of the ornaments and conveniences of life, to bodily austerities, and to serious thoughts." He finally consented, his brother Charles, Benj. Ingham and Charles Delamotte joining him.

When the project was made public it was regarded by many as a Quixotic scheme. One inquired of John[,] "Do you intend to become a knight-errant? How did Quixotism get into your head? You want nothing. You have a good provision for life. You are in a fair way for promotion, and yet you are leaving all to fight wind-mills."

"Sir," replied Mr. Wesley, "if the Bible be not true, I am as very a fool and madman as you can conceive. But if that book be of God, I am sober-minded; for it declares 'There is no man that hath left houses, and friends, and brethren, for the kingdom of God's sake, who shall not receive manifold more in this present time, and in the world to come 'everlasting life.'"

He submitted his plans to his widowed mother, asking her advice. She replied, "Had I twenty sons, I should rejoice if they were all so employed." His sister Emily said,

"Go, my brother;" and his brother Samuel joined with his mother and sister in bidding him God-speed.

All things being in readiness, on the 14th of October, 1735, the company embarked on board the *Simmonds,* off Gravesend, and after a few days detention set sail for the new world.

This was a voyage of discovery—the discovery of holiness.

"One end of leaving our native land," he says, "was not to avoid want, God having given us plenty of temporal blessings; nor to gain the dung and dross of riches and honor; but simply to save our souls; to live wholly to the glory of God."

Wesley hoped, by subjecting himself to the hardships of such a life, to secure that holiness for which his soul so ardently longed. He had no clear conception, as yet, of the doctrine of salvation by faith alone. He hoped, by spending his life among rude savages, to escape the temptations of the great metropolis. In the wilds of America he could live on "water and bread, and the fruits of the earth," and speak "without giving offense." He justly concluded that "pomp and show of the world had no place in the wilds of America." "An Indian hut offered no food for curiosity." "My chief motive," he says, "is the hope of saving my own soul. I hope to learn the true sense of the gospel of Christ by preaching it to the heathen." "I cannot hope to attain the same degree of holiness here which I do there." "I hope," he continues, "from the moment I leave the English shore, under the acknowledged character of a teacher sent from God, there shall be no word heard from my lips but what properly flows from that character."

But Wesley could not get away from himself. The greatest hindrance to holiness was in his own heart. He had looked for holiness in works, sacrifices, austerities, etc., but had failed to see that it was by faith alone.

The voyage, though of almost unparalleled roughness, was of infinite profit to Wesley. A company of Moravians, with David Nitzsehmann as their bishop, were passengers, bound to the new world, fleeing from popish persecution. Wesley, observing their behavior in the midst of great peril, was convinced that they were in possession of that to which he was a stranger. Ingham represented them as "a heavenly-minded people."

Fifty-seven days of sea life brought them within sight of the beautiful Savannah. Soon they were kneeling upon its soil, thanking God for His merciful care and providential deliverance.

Soon after landing in Georgia, Wesley met Spangenburg, the Moravian elder, and desired to know of him how he should prosecute his new enterprise. This devout man of God saw clearly the need of the young evangelist, and inquired of him: "Have you the witness within yourself? Does the Spirit of God bear witness with your spirit that you are a child of God?" Wesley seemed surprised at such a question. Spangenburg continued: "Do you know Jesus Christ?" Wesley replied: "I know Him as the Savior of the world." "True," responded the Moravian elder, "but do you know that He saves you?" Wesley replied: "I hope He has died to save me." Spangenburg gravely added: "Do you know yourself?" Wesley answered: "I do;" and here the interview ended.

Charles Wesley was Oglethorpe's secretary, in place of the Rev. Samuel Quincy, a native of Massachusetts, who retired from the office, desiring to return to England, where he had been educated. Ingham seems to have attached himself to Charles Wesley, and devoted himself to the children and the poor, and was the first to follow Charles to England. Delamotte was impelled to go to Georgia from his love of John Wesley, and his desire to serve him in any capacity; and he never left him for a day while Wesley remained in America. He was the last to leave the colony. John Wesley was the sole minister of the colony and stood next to Oglethorpe himself.

The Georgia to which Wesley came was very different from the Georgia of to-day. It had only a few English settlements, the most of the territory being the home of savage Indians. These tribes being at war with each other, all access to them was cut off. Not being able to extend their mission among them, Wesley and his co-laborers turned their attention to the whites, hoping that God would, before long, open their way to preach the gospel to the Indians. In the prosecution of their mission they practiced the most rigid austerities. They slept on the ground instead of on beds; lived on bread and water, dispensing with all the luxuries and with most of the necessaries of life. They were in season and out of season, everywhere urging the people to a holy life. Wesley set apart three hours of each day for visiting the people at their homes, choosing the midday hours when the people were kept indoors by the scorching heat.

Charles Wesley and Mr. Ingham were at Frederica, where the people were frank to declare that they liked nothing they did. Even Oglethorpe himself had become the enemy of his secretary, and falsely accused him of inciting a mutiny.

Their plain, earnest, practical public preaching and private rebukes aroused the spirit of persecution, which broke upon them without mixture of mercy. *Scandal,* with scorpion tongue, *backbiting,* with its *canine* proclivities, and *gossip,* which always does immense business on borrowed capital—these ran like fires over sun-scorched prairies, until these devoted servants of God were well-nigh consumed.

At Frederica, Charles narrowly escaped assassination. So general and bitter was the hate, that he says: "Some turned out of the way to avoid me." "The servant that used to wash my linen sent it back unwashed." "I sometimes pitied and sometimes diverted myself with the odd expressions of their contempt; but found the benefit of having undergone a much lower degree of obloquy at Oxford."

While very sick, he was unable to procure a few boards to lie upon, and was obliged to lie on the ground in the corner of Mr. Reed's hut. He thanked God that it had not as yet become a "capital offense to give him a morsel of bread." Though very sick, he was able to go out at night to bury a scout boatman, but "envied him his quiet grave." He procured the old bedstead on which the boatman had died, upon which to rest his own sinking and almost dying frame; but the bedstead was soon taken from him by order of Oglethorpe himself. But through the mercy of God and the coming of his brother and Mr. Delamotte, he recovered.

After about six months (February 5 to July 25) spent in labors more abundant, and almost in stripes above measure, Providence opened his way to return to England as bearer of dispatches to the government. He took passage in an old, rickety vessel, with a drunken captain, and all came near being lost at sea. The vessel put into Boston in distress, and there Charles Wesley remained for more than a month, preaching several times in King's Chapel, corner of School and Tremont Streets, and in Christ's Church on Salem Street. This latter church remains as it was when Wesley occupied its pulpit.

John remained in Georgia—at Frederica and Savannah—battling with sin and Satan, with a Christian boldness which might almost have inspired wonder among the angels. His life was frequently threatened at Frederica, and at Savannah there was no end to the insults he endured. Hearing of his conflicts, Whitefield writes to him to "go on and prosper, and, in the strength of God, make the devil's kingdom shake about his ears."

Through the cunning craftiness and manifest hypocrisy of one Miss Hopkey, niece of the chief magistrate, and a young lady of great external accomplishments, he was well-nigh ruined. She sought his company; bestowed on him every attention; watched him when sick; was always at his early morning meetings, dressed in pure white, because she learned that he was pleased with that color; was always manifesting great interest in her spiritual state; and all, without doubt, to cover up deeper designs. Mr. Wesley, always unsuspecting and confiding, became strongly attached to her for a time, but was subsequently convinced that God did not approve of an alliance in that direction, and at once determined to cut every cord which bound them. At this the lady became greatly exasperated, and within a few days was married to another man—Williamson—and then, with her husband and uncle to aid her, she sought in every way the overthrow of Wesley.

Mr. Tyerman seeks to make this case, as in fact many others, turn to the disadvantage of Wesley. He will have it that Wesley had promised to marry Miss Hopkey, though Henry Moore declares that Wesley told him that no such thing ever occurred. Mr. Tyerman gives credit to the testimony of the hypocritical Miss Hopkey, rather than to that of Henry Moore and John Wesley.

After a time Wesley, for just causes, excluded Mrs. Williamson from the Lord's table, and gave his reasons for so doing. For this he was prosecuted before the courts, a packed and paid grand jury bringing against him ten indictments, and the minority presenting a strong counter report. The case never came to trial, though Wesley made seven fruitless efforts to have it tried.

The prejudice excited against him by the chief magistrate and others became so strong that he could accomplish but little good among the people.

In the midst of these conflicts he held every Sunday, from five to six, a prayer service in English; at nine, another in Italian; from 10.30 to 12.30, he preached a sermon in English and administered the communion; at one he held a service in French; at two he catechised the children; at three he held another service in English; still later, he conducted a service in his own house, consisting of reading, prayer and praise; and at six attended the Moravian service.

He finally resolved, as his mission seemed at an end, to leave Georgia and return to England. His public announcement of his purpose created great excitement among all classes. The magistrate forbade his departure. Williamson demanded that he give bail to answer the suit against him; but this he refused to do, telling them that he had sought seven times to have the case tried, but in vain, and that for the balance, they could look after that. On the same night, after public prayers, with four men to accompany him, Wesley left Savannah, December 2, 1737, never more to return. They took a small boat to Perrysburgh, a distance of some twelve miles. They then made their way on foot through swamps and forests, suffering untold hardships from cold, hunger and thirst for four days, when they safely arrived at Port Royal. Here Delamotte joined them, and all took boat for Charleston, where they arrived after four more days of toil.

After spending a few days in Charleston, Mr. Delamotte returned to Savannah, and on the 22d of December, Mr. Wesley set sail for England, where he safely arrived on the first day of the following February, the next day after Mr. Whitefield had sailed for America.

Mr. Wesley did not regard his mission to America as a failure. He blessed God for having been carried to America, contrary to all his preceding resolutions. "Hereby, I trust, he hath, in some measure, *humbled me and proved me, and shown me what was in my heart.*"

Mr. Whitefield writes on his arrival in Georgia: "The

work Mr. Wesley has done in America is inexpressible. His name is very precious among the people; and he has laid a foundation that I hope neither man nor devils will ever be able to shake. O that I may follow him as he followed Christ."

Chapter III.
Wesley's Religious Experience.

Mr. Wesley's religious experience deserves special notice. If he was raised up of God for any purpose, it was to revive spiritual Christianity, which included justification by faith, the witness of the Spirit, and entire sanctification. To understand his own experience on these doctrines is the object of this chapter.

Let us first notice the external religious life which Mr. Wesley maintained prior to the wonderful change which occurred soon after his return from America. From his journal we learn that he said prayers both public and private, and read the Scriptures and other good books constantly. He experienced sensible comfort in reading Kempis, resulting in an entire change in his conversation and life. He set apart two hours each day for religious retirement, and received the sacrament every week. He watched against every sin, whether in word. or deed. He shook off all his trifling acquaintances, and was careful that every moment of his time should be improved. He not only watched over his own heart, but urged others to become religious. He visited those in prison, assisted the poor and sick, and did what he could, with his presence and means, for the souls and bodies of men. He deprived himself of all the superfluities and of many of the necessaries of life, that he might help others. He fasted twice each week, omitted no part of self-denial which he thought lawful, and carefully used in public and private, at all opportunities, all the means of grace. For the doing of these things he became a by-word, but rejoiced that his name was cast out as evil. His sole aim was to do God's will and secure inward holiness. Sometimes he had joy, sometimes sorrow; sometimes the terror of the law alarmed him, and sometimes the comforts of the Gospel cheered him. He had many remarkable answers to prayer, and many sensible soul comforts.

Let us next notice Mr. Wesley's estimate of his own religious state at this time.

He found that he had not such faith in Christ as kept his heart from being troubled in time of danger, for in a storm he cried unto God every moment, but in a calm he did not. His works he discovered to be such as did not edify, especially his manner of speaking of his enemies. By these he was convinced of unbelief and pride. He gives a dark picture of his state at this time, much darker than the light of after years justified. "I went to America," he says, "to convert the Indians, but O! who shall convert me? I have a fair summer religion. Oh, who will deliver me from this fear of death?"

On landing in England he writes: "It is now two years and almost four months since I left my native country, in order to teach the Georgia Indians the nature of Christianity; but what have I learned myself in the meantime? Why, what I least of all expected, that I, who went to America to convert others, was never myself converted to God."

He further says: "This, then, have I learned in the ends of the earth, that I am fallen short of the glory of God, alienated from the life of God, I am a child of wrath, an heir of hell."

In later years, when carefully reconsidering his early experience, Mr. Wesley was not disposed to form the same severe judgment of his religious state. He wisely added several qualifying remarks, which should not be omitted when his early language is employed. He could not say that he was not converted at this time, or that he was a child of wrath. To the expression— "I was never myself converted to God," is added this note— "I am not sure of that;" strongly intimating that he believed he was then converted.

To the expression— "I am a child of wrath, an heir of hell," is added this note— "I believe not." It seemed to his own mature judgment that he was not the wretched sinner he had fancied himself to be in these sad hours of his early history. He says, "I had then the faith of a *servant,* though not that of a *son.*" What he means by this expression may be gathered from a sermon which he preached some fifty years later. He says, "But what is the faith which is properly saving; which brings eternal salvation to all those that keep it to the end? It is such a divine conviction of God, and the things of God, as even in its infant state enables everyone that possesses it to fear God and work righteousness. And whosoever in every nation believes thus far, the Apostle declares is accepted of him. He actually is, at that very moment, in a state of acceptance. But he is at present only a *servant* of God, not properly a *son.* Meantime, let it be well observed, that the 'wrath of God,' no longer abideth on him."

"Indeed, nearly fifty years ago, when the preachers, commonly called Methodists, began to preach that grand Scriptural doctrine, salvation by faith, they were not sufficiently apprized of the difference between a servant and a child of God. They did not clearly understand that everyone who feareth God and worketh righteousness, is accepted of Him. In consequence of this, they are apt to make sad the hearts of those whom God had not made sad. For they frequently asked those who feared God, 'Do you know that your sins are forgiven?' And upon their answering 'no,' immediately replied, 'Then you are a child of the devil.' No, that does not follow. It might have been said (and it is all that can be said with propriety), 'Hitherto you are a *servant*, you are not a *child* of God.' The faith of a child is, properly and directly, a divine conviction, whereby every child of God is enabled to testify, 'The life that I now live, I live by faith in the Son of God, who loved me and gave himself for me.' And whosoever hath this, the Spirit of God witnesseth with his spirit that he is a child of God. This, then, it is that properly constitutes the difference between a servant of God and a child of God."

Again he says: "The faith of a servant implies a Divine evidence of the invisible world, so far as it can exist without living experience. Whoever has attained this, the faith of a servant, 'feareth God and escheweth evil;' or, as it is expressed by St. Peter, 'feareth God and worketh righteousness.' In consequence of which he is, in a degree, as the Apostle observes, 'accepted with him.' Elsewhere he is described in these words: 'He that feareth God and keepeth His commandments.'"

A careful examination of these quotations will convince anyone that the difference in Mr. Wesley's opinion between a *servant* and a *son* is not that one is converted and the other is not; not that one is accepted by God and the other rejected; but that one has the direct witness of the Spirit that he is a child of God, and the other has not. This was Wesley's religious state when he returned to England. He was not that lost soul, that heir of hell, which he reckoned himself to be, but an accepted servant of God, without the direct witness of the spirit to his sonship.

Meeting Peter Bohler, February 7, 1738, he (Bohler)

was made the instrument of a great blessing to his soul. Bohler was a Moravian, nine years the junior of Wesley; a most devout man, deeply versed in spiritual things, and well qualified to lead the earnest Oxford student into the path of peace. Wesley was astonished at the announcement of Bohler that true faith in Christ was inseparably attended by dominion over sin, and constant peace arising from a sense of forgiveness. He could in no way accept the doctrine until he had first examined the Scriptures, and had heard the testimony of three witnesses adduced by Bohler. But what staggered him most was the doctrine of instantaneous conversion. This he could not accept. But a careful appeal to the Bible, and the testimony of Bohler's witnesses, settled the question. Thus "this man of erudition," says Mr. Tyerman, "and almost anchorite piety, sat at the feet of this godly German like a little child, and was content to be thought a fool that he might be wise."

But the time drew near when the veil was to be rent, and he who had been for half a score of years a seeker, was to behold the glories of the inner temple. His brother Charles had already received the gift of the spirit, and Whitefield was rejoicing in the same blessing: but John still lingered. He became so oppressed with his spiritual state. that he thought of abandoning preaching; but Bohler said: "By no means. Preach faith till you have it, and then, because you have it you will preach it." So he began. He uttered strong words at St. Lawrence and St. Catherine, and was informed that he could preach no more in either place. At Great St. Helen's he spoke with such plainness that he was told he must preach no more there. At St. Ann's he spoke of free salvation by faith, and the doors of that church were closed against him. The same result attended his preaching at St. John's and St. Bennett's, until he found the words of a friend addressed to his brother, true in his own case, that "wherever you go this 'foolishness of preaching' will alienate hearts from you and open mouths against you."

The simplicity of faith staggered the youthful philosopher. Bohler, in writing of the Wesleys to Zinzendorf, says: "Our mode of believing in the Savior is so easy to Englishmen that they cannot reconcile themselves to it; if it were a little more artful, they could much sooner find their way into it."

Wesley's distress of soul continued until the 24th of May. At five in the morning of that auspicious day he opened his Testament and read: "There are given unto us exceeding great and precious promises, that by these ye may be partakers of the Divine nature." Later in the day he opened the Word and read: "Thou art not far from the kingdom of God." Having attended St. Paul's Cathedral in the afternoon, where the anthem was a great comfort to his soul, he went with great reluctance to a society meeting at night at Aldergate [*sic*] Street. There he found one reading Luther's preface to the Romans; and at about a quarter before nine, while the change which God works in the heart through faith in Christ was being described, "I felt," he says, "my heart strangely warmed. I felt I did trust in Christ—Christ alone—for salvation; and an assurance was given me that he had taken away my sins, even mine, and saved me from the law of sin and death; and I then testified openly to all there what I now felt in my heart."

From this moment a new spiritual world opened upon the mind and heart of John Wesley. He not only began at once to pray for those who had ill-used him, but openly testified to all present what God had done for his soul. And from that hour onward, for fifty-three years, he bore through the land a heart flaming with love.

In 1744, more than six years subsequent to that blessed experience at Aldergate, Mr. Wesley relates another experience which we must not overlook. It is related in these words: "In the evening while I was reading prayers at Snowfield, I found such light and strength as I never remember to have had before. I saw every thought, as well as action or word, just as it was rising in my heart, and whether it was right before God or tainted with pride or selfishness. I never knew before—I mean not at this time—what it was to be still before God. I waked the next morning by the grace of God in the same spirit; and about eight, being with two or three that believed in Jesus, I felt such an awe and tender sense of the presence of God, as greatly confirmed me therein; so that God was before me all the day long. I sought and found him in every place; and could truly say, when I lay down at night; 'now I have lived to-day.'"

In 1771, referring to this experience, he says: "Many years since I saw that 'without holiness no man shall see the Lord.' I began by following after it, and inciting all with whom I had any intercourse to do the same. Ten years after, God gave me a clearer view than I had before of the way how to attain it; namely, by faith in the Son of God. And immediately I *declared* to all, 'We are saved from sin, we are made holy by faith.' *This I testified in private, in public, in print;* and God confirmed it by a THOUSAND WITNESSES. I have continued to declare this for above thirty years; and God has continued to confirm the work of grace."

These experiences flamed out in his whole life. He claimed that he *knew whereof* he affirmed. While he advocated strongly the doctrines of Christianity, he was most earnest in promoting the experience.

Chapter IV.
Wesley's Labors.

NO SOONER HAD MR. WESLEY experienced the transforming power of grace than he hastened to declare it to all, taking the world for his parish.

After confessing to those immediately about him what God had done for his soul, he flew with all possible speed to declare it to the miners in their darkness, to the Newgate felons in their cells, to the wealthy and refined worshippers at St. John's and St. Ives; offering, in burning words, a common salvation alike to the Newgate felon and to the St. John's and St. Ives aristocracy.

Mr. Wesley was a most pertinacious adherent of the English establishment, and never dreamed of attempting the salvation of souls by preaching the gospel outside her church walls, until he was ruthlessly expelled from all her pulpits. But he had firmly resolved that neither bishops, nor curates, nor church wardens should stand between him and duty. But what to do and where to go he did not know.

In his extremity he took counsel of Whitefield, resulting in a firm purpose to do the work to which Providence seemed to have clearly called them.

Churches were closed, to be sure, but the unsaved and perishing were everywhere except in the churches, and to reach and save them they betook themselves to the wide, wide world. They were now seen in hospitals, administering spiritual comfort to the sick; in prisons, offering eternal life to condemned felons; at Kingswood, calling the dark colliers to a knowledge of the truth. In these places, unfrequented by sacerdotal robes, the gospel of the grace of God was carried by these unhonored servants of Jesus. But soon prisons and hospitals were denied them, and then they fled to the fields and to the streets of the cities, choosing for their pulpit the market-house steps, a horse block, a coal heap, a table, a stone wall, a mountain side, a horse's back, etc.

The colliers of Kingswood had no church, no Sabbath, no gospel. They were the most corrupt, degraded, blasphemous class to be found in England. Southey describes them as "lawless, brutal and worse than heathen." They seemed to have been forsaken of God and man. This was a fit place to test the power of the "gospel of the grace of God." The intrepid Whitefield was the first to break the ice. "Pulpits are denied," he says, "and the poor colliers are ready to perish." So he unfurled the banner, "With a mountain for his pulpit," he says, "and the broad heavens for a sounding-board."

The Wesleys are lifting up their voices like trumpets in all parts of the kingdom. They are threading their way along the mountains of Wales, where the people know as little of Christianity as do the wild Indians of our western forests and plains. Then they are seen in Ireland, in all her towns and cities, calling her papal cursed sons to a knowledge of Jesus. Again their voices are heard amid the hills and vales of Scotland, urging her stern clans to accept Jesus by faith alone. Then they are surrounded by tens of thousands of besmeared miners, who are weep-ing for sin and rejoicing in God. In order that the reader may get, in the briefest possible compass, some idea of the immense amount of labor performed by Mr. Wesley, we will reduce it to a few points.

1. *His travel was immense.* He averaged, during a period of fifty-four years, about five thousand miles a year, making in all some two hundred and ninety thousand miles, a distance equal to circumnavigating the globe about twelve times. It must not be forgotten that most of this travel was on horseback. Think of riding around the globe on horseback twelve times!

2. *His preaching was immense.* Mr. Wesley preached not less than twenty sermons a week—frequently many more. These sermons were delivered mostly in the open air, and under circumstances such as to test the nerve of the most vigorous frame. He did, in the matter of preaching, what no other man ever did. He preached, all an average, for a period of fifty-four years, fifteen sermons a week, making in all forty-two thousand four hundred, besides numberless exhortations and addresses on a great variety of occasions.

A minister in these times does well to preach one hundred sermons a year. At this rate, to preach as many sermons as Mr. Wesley did, such a minister must live four hundred and twenty-four years. Think of a minister preaching two sermons each week-day, and three each Sabbath, for fifty-four years, and some idea can be formed of Wesley's labors in this department.

3. *His literary labors were immense.* While traveling five thousand miles a year, or about fourteen miles a day, and preaching two sermons, and frequently five each clay, he read extensively. He read not less than one thousand two hundred volumes, on all subjects, many of the volumes *folios,* after the old English style. His journals show that he read not only to understand, but to severely criticise his author as well.

He wrote *grammars* of the Hebrew, Greek, Latin, French and English languages.

He was for many years editor of a monthly periodical of fifty-six pages, known as the *Arminian Magazine.*

He rewrote, abridged, revised and published a library of fifty volumes; and afterwards re-read, revised and republished the whole work in thirty volumes.

He wrote and published a commentary on the whole Bible, in four large volumes; but the portion on the Old Testament was rendered almost worthless by the abridgment of the notes by the printer, in order to get them within a given compass.

He compiled a complete dictionary of the English language, much used in its day.

He wrote and published a work on Natural Philosophy in five volumes, which for many years was a textbook among ministers.

He compiled a work on Ecclesiastical History in four volumes.

He wrote and published comprehensive histories of England and Rome.

He wrote a good-sized work on electricity.

He prepared and published three medical works for the common people: one, entitled Primitive Physic was highly esteemed in the old country.

He compiled and published six volumes of church music.

His poetical works, in connection with those of his brother Charles, are said to have amounted to not less than forty volumes. Charles composed the larger part, but they passed under the revision of John, without which we doubt if Charles Wesley's hymns would have been what they are, the most beautiful and soul-inspiring in the English language.

In addition to all this, there are seven large octavo volumes of sermons, letters, controversial papers, Journals, etc. It is said that Mr. Wesley's works, including abridgments and translations, amounted to some two hundred volumes.

4. *His pastoral labors were immense.* It is doubtful if any pastor in these times does more pastoral work than did Mr. Wesley. He speaks frequently of these labors. In London he visits all the members, and from house to house exhorts and comforts them. For some time he visited all the *Bands* and the *Select Societies,* appointing all the class and band leaders. He had under his special care tens of thousands of souls.

To these multiplied labors he added the establishment of schools, building of chapels, raising of funds to carry on the work, and a special care over the whole movement. It may be affirmed that neither in his travels, his literary labors, his preaching, nor in his pastoral supervision of the flock of Christ, has he often, if ever, been surpassed. Few men could have traveled as much as he, had they omitted all else. Few could have preached as much without either travel or study; and few could have written and published as much had they avoided both travel and preaching. It is not too much to say that among uninspired men, one of more extraordinary character than John Wesley never lived.

It may be asked, how was he able to accomplish so much? He improved every moment of every day to the very best advantage.

Mr. Fletcher, who for some time was his traveling companion, says: "His diligence is matchless. Though oppressed with the weight of seventy years, and the care of more than thirty thousand souls, he shames still, by his unabated zeal and immense labors, all the young ministers of England, perhaps of Christendom. He has generally blown the gospel trumpet and rode twenty miles before most of the professors, who despise his labors, have left their downy pillows. As he begins the day, the week, the year, so he concludes them, still intent upon extensive services for the glory of the Redeemer and the good of souls."

In order to save time he, in the first place, ascertained how much sleep he needed; and when once settled, he never varied from it to the end of life. He arose at four o'clock in the morning, and retired at ten in the evening, never losing at any time, he says, ten minutes by wakefulness. The first hour of each day was devoted to private devotions; then every succeeding hour and moment were employed in earnest labor. His motto was, "Always in haste, but never in a hurry." "I have," he says, "no time to be in a hurry. Leisure and I have taken leave of each other."

He makes the remarkable statement that "ten thousand cares were no more weight to his mind than ten thousand hairs to his head." "I am never tired with writing, preaching, or traveling."

With all his travel, labor and care, he declares that he "enjoyed more hours of private retirement than any man in England." When it is remembered that all this labor was performed amid the most unrelenting persecution that ever fell to the lot of man in modern times, it must be confessed that John Wesley has had no superior among uninspired men.

Chapter V.
Wesley's Persecutions.

HAD THE IMMENSE LABORS of John Wesley, noticed in the preceding chapter, been performed under public patronage, cheered on by all, they would have seemed less arduous. Men may prosecute a reform, when public opinion favors it, with comparative ease, but with less entitlement to honor than he has a right to claim who does it in the face of passion and interest. The labors of John Wesley were prosecuted in the teeth of opposition such as seldom falls to the lot of man to endure. And what made it more dastardly and cruel was the fact that it was instigated and principally conducted by the officials of that church of which he was a worthy member and ordained minister to the day of his death.

It is a sad fact, but nevertheless true, that most of the opposition and persecution encountered by reformers and revivalists has come from the churchmen of the times. It has been the church opposing those who were honestly seeking her own reformation. When the church substitutes forms for godliness, and devotes herself to ecclesiasticism instead of to soul-saving, and place-seeking takes the place of piety, she is ready to resist all efforts for her restoration to spirituality as irregular and offensive.

No sooner had Wesley exposed the sins of the church, especially those of the pulpit, than the pulpit denounced him; and the press taking its keynote from the pulpit, thundered as though the end of the world had come. Then the idle rabble rushed to the front, and mob violence and mob law was the order of the hour.

The flaming denunciations of the pulpits of the establishment against Mr. Wesley and his people have never been surpassed in the history of the English nation. Wesley says, "We were everywhere represented as mad dogs and treated accordingly. In sermons, newspapers and pamphlets of all kinds, we were painted as unheard-of monsters. But this moved us not; we went on testifying salvation by faith, both to small and great, and not counting our lives dear unto ourselves, so we might finish our course with peace."

The Wesleys were represented as "bold movers of sedition, and ring-leaders of the rabble, to the disgrace of their order." They were denounced by learned divines as "restless deceivers of the people," "babblers," "insolent pretenders," "men of spiritual slight and cunning craftiness." They were guilty of "indecent, false and unchristian reflections on the clergy." They were "new-fangled teachers," "rash, uncharitable censurers," "intruding into other men's labors," and running "into wild fancies until the pale of the church is too strait for them." They were "half-dissenters *in* the church and more dangerous *to* the church than those who were total dissenters from it."

Bishop Gibson declared that they endeavored "to justify their own extraordinary methods of teaching by casting unworthy reflections upon the parochial clergy, as deficient in the discharge of their duty, and not instructing their people in the true doctrines of Christianity."

Even Dr. Doddridge is not at all "satisfied with the high

pretences they make to the divine influence." Dr. Trapp is bold in pronouncing them "a set of crack-brained enthusiasts, and profane hypocrites."

The *Weekly Miscellany* denounces Wesley as the "ringleader, fomenter, and first cause of all divisions and feuds that have happened in Oxford, London, Bristol, and other places where he has been." He manages by "preaching, bookselling, wheedling and sponging, to get, it is believed, an income of £700 a year, some say £1,000. This is priestcraft to perfection."

Further on in life he is accused of "making unwarrantable dissensions in the church," and "prejudicing the people wherever he comes, against his brethren, the clergy." He is a "sower and ringleader of dissension, endeavoring, with unwearied assiduity, to set the flock at variance with their ministers and each other," assuming to himself "great wisdom and high attainments in all spiritual knowledge." "You go," says this writer, "from one end of the nation to another, lamenting the heresies of your brethren, and instilling into the people's minds that they are led into error by their pastors."

"It was Mr. Wesley's fidelity," says Mr. Tyerman, "far more than the novelties of his doctrines and proceedings, that brought upon him the persecution he encountered."

The former friends of Wesley now turned against him on points merely doctrinal. No one can read the invectives of Sir Richard and Rev. Rowland Hill, Sir Walter Shirley and Rev. Augustus Toplady, without feelings of great astonishment. When Mr. Wesley had passed his three-score and ten years, Mr. Toplady, a young man of thirty, attacked him in the most violent manner, employing epithets of the most abusive character. We select the following as samples of the many. Wesley is accused of the "sophistry of the Jesuit, and the dictatorial authority of a Pope." He is a "lurking, sly assassin," guilty of "audacity and falsehood;" a "knave," guilty of "mean, malicious impotence." He is an "Ishmaelite," a "bigot," a "papist," a "defamer," a "reviler," a "liar," without the "honesty of a heathen;" an "impudent slanderer;" with "Satanic guilt only exceeded by Satan himself, if even by him." He is an "echo of Satan."

Robert Hall well said, "I would not incur the guilt of that violent abuse which Toplady cast upon him (Wesley), for points merely speculative and of very little importance, for ten thousand worlds."

Poets who should have sung for Jesus prostituted their gifts and burdened their songs with the bitterest invectives against Wesley and his people.

One entitles his poem *"Perfection:* a practical epistle, calmly addressed to the greatest hypocrite in England—that person being John Wesley."

Another poem was entitled *"Methodism* displayed: A satire, illustrated and verified from John Wesley's fanatical Journals."

Another entitled *"The Mechanic Inspired";* or, The Methodists' Welcome to Rome." As a specimen of this delectable production we give the following stanza:

> "Ye dupes of sly, Romish, itinerant liars:
> The spawn of French prophets and mendicant
>   friars;
> Ye pious enthusiastics! who riot and rob,
> With holy grimace, and sanctified sob."

Another, *"The Methodist and Mimic."*

Still another, *"The Methodist,* a poem." In this production Mr. Wesley is described as being nursed on "demoniac milk," and as one who

> "Had Moorfield trusted to his care,
> For Satan keeps an office there."

Another entitled *"The Troublers of Israel;* in which the principles of those who turn the world upside down are displayed."

Another, in which the writer exhorts Wesley to

> "Haste hence to Rome, thy proper place,
> Why should we share in thy disgrace?
> We need no greater proof to see,
> Thy blasphemies with his agree."

And yet another entitled *"Wesley's Apostacy,"* etc., in which occurs this verse, among others equally bad:

> "In vain for worse may Wesley search the globe,
> A viper hatched beneath the harlot's robe;
> Rome in her glory has no greater boast,
> Than Wesley aims—to all conviction lost."

This may answer for the poets, though their number is nearly legion.

Artists employed their God-given powers in traducing Wesley and his people.

Wm. Hogarth published a painting and engraving entitled *"Credulity, Superstition and Fanaticism,* being a satire on Methodism."

Comedians, who are generally ready to lend themselves to any vile work, employed the stage to blacken the character of Wesley.

Samuel Foote, an actor, wrote a play entitled *"The Minor,* a Comedy," in which the Methodists were ridiculed and slandered.

Samuel Pottinger wrote a play entitled *"The Methodist,* a Comedy." Another was soon after produced— *"The Hypocrite,* a Comedy, as it was performed in the Theater Royal, Drury Lane."

Thus pulpit, press, pencil and stage united to crush

Wesley and his people. No means were left untried. Though they followed him through all his active, ministerial life, yet the gates of hell did not and could not prevail against him and his work.

Mob Violence.

When pulpit, press and stage combine to crush vital Christianity, they soon arouse an ally in the ignorant, restless, unholy masses, ever ready to aid in forwarding the work of the Prince of darkness.

When pulpits in London, Bristol, Bath, and, in fact, everywhere, were closed against Wesley, one of two ways was open before him: he must either abandon the work to which he was sure God had called him, or he must break over ecclesiastical rules and go outside the churches. He was not long choosing.

A good-sized volume could be filled with accounts of mob violence which came upon Wesley and his people, but we have space for a few cases only, which must be taken as samples of the many.

While preaching at Moorfield a mob met him, broke down the table on which he stood, and in various ways abused and insulted him. Nothing daunted he mounted a stone wall nearby and exhorted the people until silence was restored. He often found himself here in the midst of a sea of human passion, the crowds frequently numbering from twenty to forty thousand.

At Sheffield, hell from beneath seemed moved to meet him at his coming. As he was wont to do, he took his stand out of doors and faced the crowd. In the midst of his sermon a military officer rushed upon him, brandishing a sword and threatening his life. Wesley faced him, threw open his breast and bade him do as he liked. The officer cowered.

The preaching house was subsequently nearly demolished over the heads of the devout worshippers. Wesley says, "It was a glorious time. Many found the spirit of glory and of God resting upon them." The next day, nothing daunted, he was in the midst of the town preaching the great salvation. The mob assembled, followed him to his lodgings, smashed in the windows and threatened to take his life. But while the mob were howling without like beasts of prey, Wesley was so little disturbed that he fell into a quiet slumber.

At Wednesbury an organized mob went to nearly all the Methodist families in town, beating and otherwise abusing men, women and children. They spoiled their wearing apparel, cut open their beds, and scattered the contents, leaving whole families houseless and homeless in midwinter and under the peltings of a pitiless storm. The people were informed that if they would sign a paper agreeing never to read or sing or pray together, or hear the Methodists preach again, their houses should not be demolished. A few complied, but the greater number answered, "We have already lost our goods, and nothing more can follow but the loss of our lives, which we will lose also rather than wrong our consciences."

A few days after, Wesley rode boldly into Wednesbury, and in a public park in the center of the town proclaimed to an immense crowd, "Jesus, the same yesterday, to-day and forever." The mob assembled, arrested him, and dragged him before a magistrate who inquired, "What have Mr. Wesley and the Methodists done?"

"Why, plaze your worship," cried one, "they sing psalms all day and make folks get up at five o'clock in the morning; now what would your worship advise us to do?" "Go home," replied the magistrate, "and be quiet."

Not satisfied with this, they hurried him off to another magistrate. A few friends followed, but were soon beaten back by a Walsal mob, which rushed upon them like wild beasts. All but four of Wesley's friends were vanquished. These stood by him to the last. One of these was a brave woman, whose English blood boiled over. She is said to have knocked down four Walsal men, one after another, and would have laid them all sprawling at her feet had not four brawny men seized and held her while a fifth beat her, until they were quite ashamed to be seen, five men beating one woman.

The mob tried to throw Wesley down that they might trample him under their feet. They struck at him with clubs, and must have nearly killed him had they hit him. They cried, "Knock his brains out," "Drown him," "Kill the dog," "Throw him into the river." One cried, "Crucify him, crucify him."

During all this time Wesley was calm. It only came into his mind, he says, that if they should throw him into the river it might spoil the papers in his pocket. He finally escaped out of their hands, and meeting his brother at Nottingham, Charles says, that he "looked like a soldier of Christ. His clothes were torn to tatters." Subsequently, the leader of that mob was converted, and being asked by Charles Wesley what he thought of his brother, "I think," said he, "that he was a *mon* of God, and God was with him, when so many of us could not kill one *mon.*"

While preaching at Roughlee, a drunken rabble assembled, led on by a godless constable. Wesley was arrested and taken before a magistrate. On the way he was struck on the face and head, and clubs were flourished about his person with threats of murder. The justice demanded that he promise not to come to Roughless again. Wesley answered that he would sooner cut off his head than make such a promise. As he departed from the magistrate, the mob followed, cursing him and throwing stones. Wesley was beaten to the earth, and forced back into the house. "Mr. Mackford, who came with Mr. Wesley from Newcastle, was dragged by the hair of his head, and sustained injuries from which he never fully recovered." Some of the Methodists present were beaten with clubs, others trampled in the mire; one was forced to leap from a rock ten or twelve feet high into the river, and others escaped with their lives under a shower of missiles. The magistrate witnessed all this with apparent satisfaction, without any attempt to stay the murderous tide.

These are examples of what occurred almost daily, and that for many years. At Pool, at Litchfield, at Bristol, at St. Ives, at Grimsby, at Cork, at Wendlock, at Athlone, at Dudley, and at many other places he encountered similar opposition, until the presence of a Methodist preacher was the signal for a mob. Many of the preachers were impressed into the army, on the pretense that their occupation was irregular and their lives vagabondish. But wherever they were, they were true to God and to the faith as they felt it in their hearts.

The cause of all this opposition was the preaching of justification by faith, entire sanctification, and the urging of clergy and laity to a holy life. Thomas Oliver tells Richard Hill that the man he had maligned was one who had published a hundred volumes, who had traveled yearly five thousand miles, preached yearly about one thousand sermons, visited as many sick beds as he had preached sermons, and written twice as many letters; and who, though now between seventy and eighty years of age, absolutely refused to abate, in the smallest degree, these mighty labors; but might be seen at this very time, with his silver locks about his ears, and with a meager, worn-out, skeleton body, smiling at storms and tempests, at such difficulties and dangers as "I believe," says Oliver, "would be absolutely intolerable to *you,* sir, in conjunction with any four of *your* most flaming ministers."

Such is John Wesley in his persecutions. Who would be ready to follow in his footsteps? The world needs a few such men in it now. The man who tells the whole truth will be maligned, and traduced, and misrepresented, as was Wesley; but the grace of God and the necessity for the work should urge all to duty.

Chapter VI.
Wesley as a Man, a Preacher, and a Reformer.

BEFORE WE PROCEED FURTHER with the life of this extraordinary man, let us pause long enough to take a look at his person.

We have always more or less curiosity to know the personal appearance of distinguished characters.

We are told that Mr. Wesley's figure was, in all respects, remarkable. He was low of stature, with a habit of body always the reverse of corpulent, indicative of strict temperance and continual exercise. His step was firm, and his appearance vigorous and muscular. His face, even in old age, is described as remarkably fine, a clear, smooth forehead, an aquiline nose, an eye, the brightest and most piercing that could be conceived; with a freshness of complexion scarcely ever found in a man of his years, giving him a venerable and interesting appearance. In him cheerfulness was mingled with gravity, and sprightliness with serene tranquillity.

In dress he was a pattern of neatness and simplicity, with a narrow plaited stock, a coat with a small upright collar, with no silk or velvet on any part of his apparel— these, added to a head as white as snow, gave to the beholder an idea of something primitive and apostolic.

The following description of him is given by one who, though not a Methodist, could properly appreciate true greatness.

"Very lately, I had an opportunity, for some days together, of observing Mr. Wesley with attention. I endeavored to consider him, not so much with an eye of a friend, as with the impartiality of a philosopher; and I must declare, every hour I spent in his company, afforded me fresh reasons for esteem and veneration. So fine an old man I never saw. The happiness of his mind beamed forth in his countenance; every look showed how fully he enjoyed 'The gay remembrance of a life well spent.' Wherever he went, he diffused a portion of his own felicity. Easy and affable in his demeanor, he accommodated himself to every sort of company, and showed how happily the most finished courtesy may be blended with the most perfect piety.

"In his conversation, we might be at a loss whether to admire most his fine classical taste, his extensive knowledge of men and things, or his overflowing goodness of heart. In him, even old age appeared delightful, like an evening without a cloud; and it was impossible to observe him without wishing fervently, *May my latter end be like his!* For my own part, I never was so happy as while with him, and scarcely ever felt more poignant regret at parting with him; for well I knew 'I never should look upon his like again.' "

Having looked upon the man, we will next consider him in two aspects.

1. *As a preacher.* Mr. Wesley was styled "the mover of men's consciences." His preaching was simple—a child could easily understand him. There were no far-fetched terms—no soaring among the clouds. All was simple, artless and clear. He declares that he would

no sooner preach a fine sermon than he would wear a fine coat.

George Whitefield was regarded as the prince of modern eloquence. Dr. Franklin, no mean judge, accorded him this rank. Charles Wesley was but little inferior to Whitefield as a pulpit orator; while Fletcher was not inferior to either; Mr. Wesley regarded him as superior to Whitefield. "He had," says Wesley, "a more striking person, equally good breeding and winning address; together with a rich flow of fancy, a strong understanding, and a far greater treasure of learning, both in language, philosophy, philology and divinity, and above all (which I can speak with fuller assurance, because I had a thorough knowledge both of one and the other), a more deep and constant communion with the Father, and with His Son, Jesus Christ."

These were mighty men. The multitudes which listened to them were swayed by their eloquence and power as the forest is by a rushing mighty wind. Their earnest appeals drew floods of tears from eyes unaccustomed to weep.

We are not informed that Mr. Wesley often wept while preaching, and yet no such effects were produced by Whitefield's preaching as were witnessed under Wesley's. Mr. Southey admits that the sermons of Wesley were attended with greater and more lasting effect than were the sermons of Whitefield. Men fell under his words like men in battle. While he was calm, collected, deliberate and logical, he was more powerful in moving the sensibilities as well as the understanding of his hearers, than any other man in England. Marvellous were the physical effects produced by his preaching.

We are told that "his attitude in the pulpit was graceful and easy; his action, calm and natural, yet pleasing and expressive; his voice not loud, but clear, agreeable and masculine; his style, neat and perspicuous."

His command over an audience was very remarkable. He always faced the mob, and was generally victorious at such times. In the midst of a mob he says, "I called for a chair; the winds were hushed, and all was calm and still; my heart was filled with love, my eyes with tears, and my mouth with arguments. They were amazed, they were ashamed, they were melted down, they devoured every word." There must have been, in such preaching, that which seldom falls to our lot to hear.

Beattie once heard him preach at Aberdeen one of his ordinary sermons. He remarked that "it was not a masterly sermon, yet none but a master could have preached it."

2. *Wesley as a Reformer.* Those moral reformers who have shaken nations, and in some cases revolutionized governments, were quite unknown in the days of Wesley. He was at least a hundred years in advance of his time.

1. *Slavery.* The English government, in the time of Wesley, was strongly wedded to slavery. She had enriched herself from the African slave trade. Her great maritime cities were built on the bones, sinews and flesh, cemented by the blood of oppressed bondmen. To oppose slavery was to oppose the government.

Wesley met this gigantic evil like a Christian reformer. He united with Clarkson, Wilberforce and others to oppose the evil. He represents the African slave trade as "the sum of all villainies." American slavery, he declares, was the "vilest that ever saw the sun." He had seen it, and he spoke from personal knowledge. No addresses ever made on the subject, during the days of greatest excitement, exceeded in severity those which fell from his lips.

His last letter written only four days before his death, was addressed to Wilberforce, urging him to persevere in the work. It is as follows:

London, Feb. 26, 1791.

Dear Sir:—Unless the Divine power has raised you up to be an *Athanasius Contra Numdum* (Athanasius against the world), I see not how you can go through your glorious enterprise, in opposing that execrable villainy, which is the scandal of religion, of England, and of human nature. Unless God has raised you up for this very thing, you will be worn out by the opposition of men and devils. But "if God be for you, who can be against you?" Are all of them together stronger than God? O, "be not weary in well doing." Go on, in the name of God, and in the power of His might, till even American Slavery (the vilest that ever saw the sun) shall vanish away before it.

Reading this morning a tract, written by a poor African, I was particularly struck by that circumstance,—that a man who has a black skin, being wronged or outraged by a white man, can have no redress; it being a law, in all our colonies, that the oath of a black against a white goes for nothing. What villainy is this!

That He who has guided you from your youth up, may continue to strengthen you in this and all things, is the prayer of, dear sir, Your affectionate servant,

John Wesley.

2. With reference to *Temperance* he was still farther in advance of his time than in the matter of slavery. Liquor drinking was practiced by all classes, from the Archbishop down to the meanest street scavengers. Ministers by scores drank to drunkenness, and in their drunken sprees would lead mobs against Wesley and his helpers. Wesley thundered away at liquor selling like a modern prohibition lecturer. Take the following from one of his sermons as an example:

"Neither may we gain by hurting our neighbor in his

body. Therefore, we may not sell anything which tends to impair his health. Such is eminently, all that liquor fire, called drams of spirituous liquors. It is true, they may have a place in medicine; may be used in some bodily disorders; although there would rarely be occasion for them were it not for the unskillfulness of the practitioner. Therefore, such as prepare and sell them only for this end, may keep their consciences clean. But who are they who prepare and sell them only for this end? Do you know ten distillers in England? Then excuse these. But all who sell them in the common way to any that will buy, are poisoners in general. They murder his majesty's subjects by wholesale; neither do their eyes pity or spare. They drive them to hell like sheep. And what is their gain? Is it not the blood of these men? Who, then, would enjoy their large estate and sumptuous palaces? A curse is in the midst of them. A curse cleaves to the stones, the timbers, the furniture of them! The curse of God is in their gardens, their walks, their groves; a fire that burns to the nethermost hell! Blood, blood is there! The foundation, the walls, the roof are stained with blood! And canst thou hope, O man of blood, though thou art 'clothed in scarlet and fine linen, and farest sumptuously every day,' canst thou hope to deliver down thy *fields of blood* to the third generation? Not so! There is a God in heaven; therefore thy name shall be blotted out. Like as those whom thou hast destroyed, body and soul, thy memory shall perish with thee."—*Wesley's Works,* Vol. i., p. 344.

He introduced into his discipline a rule prohibiting the "buying or selling of spirituous liquors, or drinking them, unless in cases of extreme necessity." He went for *"prohibiting forever, making a full end* of that bane of health, that destroyer of strength, of life and virtue—*distilling."* These are his own words. He was a prohibitionist in principle—and in this respect was in advance of many would-be temperance men of these times. To one of his preachers he says, "Touch no dram. It is a liquid fire. It is a sure, though slow, poison. It saps the very springs of life."

He even went so far as to attack tobacco. He exhorts, "Use no tobacco. It is an uncleanly and unwholesome self-indulgence; and the more customary it is, the more resolutely should you break off from every degree of that evil custom.

"Let Christians be in this bondage no longer. Assert your liberty, and that all at once; nothing will be done by degrees."—*Works,* Vol. vi., p. 746.

Such were the teachings of John Wesley on these subjects of reform—teachings which we regard as very remarkable for those times, and as fully up to the present.

Chapter VII.
The Closing Scene.

THOUGH PERSECUTION AND OPPOSITION followed John Wesley from the day he lifted up a standard of holiness within the classic walls of Oxford, to the hour that God's chariot bore him to the city of the great King, he never faltered in his purpose, nor abated his zeal for an hour. As his end grew near, the opposition which had been so relentless began to give way. In many places it became greatly modified, and in others nearly extinct. That a great change had come began to be manifest in public opinion and feeling. Mob violence, which once swept everything, had entirely subsided, and towns and cities which once welcomed him with brickbats and rotten eggs, now hailed him as the greatest of modern evangelists. Many who bade him depart out of their coasts as a crazy fanatic, now thought it an honor to welcome him as the man of many virtues and unparalleled labors.

Wesley outlived all his early colaborers. He saw them fall, one by one, until he stood alone of them all, waiting and watching, but pressing toward the mark for the prize.

The first to fall was the zealous, the deeply consecrated, the profoundly intellectual Walsh, at the age of twenty-eight; one of the best Biblical scholars of his day. His last words were, "He's come! He's come!" and a cloud received him from human sight.

Next to follow was the earnest, fearless, honest Grimshaw, exclaiming, "I am as happy as I can be in this world, and as sure of heaven as though I was there. I have my foot on the threshold already."

Next fell Whitefield, in America, one of the most eloquent and effective preachers that ever lifted up his voice among men.

Next followed the amiable, venerable Perronet, whom Charles Wesley was wont to call "The Archbishop of Methodism."

Then fell the most saintly man of his time—the seraphic Fletcher; shouting, "God is love!" "O for a gust of praise to go to the ends of the earth!"

Next came the sad tidings of the death of his brother Charles, but little, if any, inferior to Whitefield as a preacher, and whose sacred lyrics will live so long as human hearts are melted and charmed by the power of song. Just before the silver cord was loosed, he requested his wife to write. It was his last.

"In age, and feebleness extreme
Who shall a helpless worm redeem?
Jesus, my only hope Thou art—
Strength of my failing flesh and heart;
O could I catch a smile from Thee,
And drop into eternity."

Thus friend after friend departed, but Wesley pressed forward, with a zeal which knew no abatement until eighty and eight years had passed over him.

On his last birthday he writes: "This day I enter into my eighty-eighth year. For above eighty-six years, I found none of the infirmities of old age; my eye did not wax dim, neither was my natural strength abated. But last August I found almost a sudden change; my eyes were so dim that no glasses would help me; my strength likewise quite forsook me, and probably will not return in this world. But I feel no pain from head to foot; only it seems nature is exhausted, and, humanly speaking, will sink more and more, till

> 'The weary wheels of life stand still at last.'"

He attended and presided at his last Conference held at Bristol, July 26, 1790. Anxious to devote every hour and moment to the service of the Master, he visits Cornwall, London, and the Isle of Wight, and then returns to Bristol. He is again in London; and then he is seen standing under the shade of a large tree at Winchelsea, preaching his last out-door sermon. Though unable longer to preach in the open air, he still continues to preach "the glorious gospel of the blessed God." At Colchester, rich and poor, clergy and laity, throng to hear him, in wondering crowds. At Norwich, where once mob violence swept everything, he is received as an angel of mercy. At Yarmouth the house is thronged. At Lynn all the clergy in the town, save a lame one, come out to hear him.

Again he is in London, preaching in all his chapels, and even making preparations to visit Ireland and Scotland. But these last visits his failing strength will not allow.

The shadows are lengthening, and he seems conscious that his end is near. He preaches his last sermon at Leatherhead, Wednesday, February 3, 1791, from Isa. 55:6, "Seek ye the Lord while he may be found, call ye upon him while he is near." He concluded the sermon by singing one of Charles Wesley's hymns:

"O that without a lingering groan,
I may the welcome word receive;
My body with my charge lay down,
And cease at once to work and live."

On that day fell from his lips a gospel trumpet, which had sounded the word of life more frequently and effectually than was ever known to have been done by an uninspired man.

The dying hour came. The Christian warrior of forty-two thousand battles is about to lay aside his armor and retire to rest.

Looking over the whole of an extended life of unparalleled labor and suffering, he exclaims:

"I the chief of sinners am,
But Jesus died for me."

The day following he was heard to say: "There is no way into the holiest, but by the blood of Jesus."

He frequently, with full heart, sang his rapturous hymn, beginning:

"I'll praise my Maker while I've breath."

The tide of life is rapidly ebbing, but light from the realms above reveals to his enraptured soul the glories of his eternal home. Collecting all his remaining strength, he joyfully exclaims:

"The best of all is, God is with us."

The chamber where the good man gathers up his feet in death seemed radiant with the Divine glory. A few of his preachers and intimate friends were there—Bradford, long his traveling companion; Whitehead, afterwards his biographer; Rogers and his devoted wife, Hester Ann, who ministered to Wesley in his last hours; the daughter of Charles Wesley, and a few others. They knelt around his couch; Bradford prayed, and the dying saint exclaimed: "I'll praise! I'll praise!" Then with a low but almost angelic whisper he said, "Farewell!" It was his last; and while they lingered in silent pleading, without a struggle or a sigh,

"The weary wheels of life stood still,"

and the unparalleled career of John Wesley was ended, March 2, 1791.

Hester Ann Rogers, who was present, says: "A cloud of the Divine presence rested on all; and while he could hardly be said to be an inhabitant of earth, being now speechless, and his eyes fixed, victory and glory were written on his countenance, and quivered, as it were, on his dying lips. No language can paint what appeared in that face! The more we gazed upon it, the more we saw heaven unspeakable."

Thus lived and died the founder of the Methodist denomination.

Conclusion.

We have followed Mr. Wesley through some portions of his eventful life to its close. We have seen him pass within the veil with a glory almost ineffable. It only remains to say a few words with regard to his burial and his character.

He had requested in his will, and, in the name of God, most solemnly adjured his executors scrupulously to observe it: that six poor men should carry his body to the grave, and should receive one pound each for the same.

He requested that there should be no display, no hearse, no coach, no escutcheon, no pomp, except the tears of those who loved him and were following him to Abraham's bosom. All these directions were strictly observed.

Mr. Wesley's death attracted public notice beyond any former example, not only in London, but throughout the United Kingdom. Thousands of his people, with the traveling preachers, went into mourning for him. The pulpits of the Methodists and of many other denominations were draped in black, and hundreds of sermons were preached on the subject of his death.

His indefatigable zeal had long been witnessed by all classes; but his motives had been variously estimated. Some attributed it to love of popularity, others to ambition, and others to love of wealth; but it now appeared that he was actuated by a pure regard for the immortal interests of mankind. Many ministers, both of the establishment and among dissenters, spoke with great respect of his long, laborious, devoted and useful life, and earnestly exhorted their hearers to follow him as he followed Christ.

"He was a man," says Lord Macaulay, "whose eloquence and logical acuteness might have rendered him eminent in literature; whose genius for government was not inferior to that of Richelieu; and who devoted all his powers, in defiance of obloquy and derision, to what he sincerely considered the highest good of his species."

The ardor of his spirit was never dampened by difficulties, nor subdued by age. The world ascribed this to enthusiasm, but he ascribed it to the grace of God. Whatever it was, it has commanded the respect of the present generation. He who was expelled from all the churches as a madman and a fanatic is now deemed worthy of a most eligible niche in England's grandest cathedral.

Dr. Watts' admirable elegy on Thomas Gouge has been applied to the death of Wesley.

"The muse that mourns a Nation's fall,
Should wait at Wesley's funeral;
Should mingle majesty and groans,
Such as she sings to sinking thrones;
And in deep sounding numbers tell,
How Zion trembled when this pillar fell;
Zion grows weak, and England poor,
Nature herself, with all her store,
Can furnish such a pomp for death no more."

"A greater poet may rise than Homer or Milton," says Dr. Dobbins, "a greater theologian than Calvin, a greater philosopher than Bacon, a greater dramatist than any of ancient or modern fame; but a more distinguished revivalist of the churches than John Wesley, never."

"Taking him altogether," says Mr. Tyerman, "Wesley is a man *sui generis*. He stands alone; he has no successor; no one like him went before; no contemporary was a co-equal. There was a wholeness about the man, such as is rarely seen. His physique, his genius, his wit, his penetration, his judgment, his memory, his beneficence; his religion, his diligence, his conversation, his courteousness, his manners, his dress—made him as perfect as we ever expect man to be on this side heaven." He arose with the lark, traveled with the sun, preached through three kingdoms like an angel, claimed the world for his parish, and died like a hero, shouting, "The best of all is, God is with us."

When will earth witness his like again?

Part Second
Wesley's Doctrine

Chapter VIII.
Christian Perfection.

The Doctrine Defined.

HAVING SKETCHED, BRIEFLY, THE life of John Wesley, we come now to consider the doctrine peculiar to his ministry, and to the system of religious truth which he formulated. This was the doctrine of Christian perfection, or entire sanctification. It was the peculiar doctrine which his opponents charged him with preaching. They said, "This is Mr. Wesley's doctrine! He preaches perfection!" "He does," responds Wesley, "yet this is not *his* doctrine any more than it is yours, or any one's else, that is a minister of Christ. For it is His doctrine, peculiarly, emphatically His; it is the doctrine of Jesus Christ. Those are His words not mine; 'Ye shall, therefore, be perfect, as your father who is in heaven is perfect.' And who says ye shall not; or, at least, not till your soul is separated from your body?"

It must not be understood that this was the only doctrine which Wesley emphasized, but it was the boast of

Wesley and the early Methodists that this was "the grand depositum which God had lodged with the people called Methodists, and for the sake of propagating this chiefly, he appears to have raised them up."

Our purpose is to set forth this doctrine, in its various aspects, as taught by Mr. Wesley, and to guard some points which have been misrepresented.

While "Christian perfection" was a common term employed by Mr. Wesley, to describe the doctrine of entire holiness, it was not the only term he used. He frequently employed other terms, such as, "perfect love," "full salvation," "full sanctification," "the whole image of God," "second change," "second blessing," "entire salvation," "clean heart," "the root of sin taken away," "cleansed from all sin," etc.

A few extracts will show how these terms were used. He says, "The moment a sinner is justified, his heart is cleansed in a low degree; but yet he has not a 'clean heart' in the full, proper sense, till he is made 'perfect in love.'" Vol. v., p. 284. Here the terms "a pure heart," and "perfect love" are used synonomously.

"I met again with those who believe God has 'delivered them from the root of bitterness.'"

To Joseph Benson: "With all zeal and diligence confirm the brethren. 1. In holding fast that whereunto they have attained; namely, the remission of all their sins, by faith in a bleeding Lord. 2. In expecting a 'second change,' whereby they shall be 'saved from all sin,' and 'perfected in love.'"—Vol. vii., p. 71.

"'Entire sanctification,' or Christian perfection, is neither more nor less than 'pure love'; love expelling sin, and governing both the heart and life of a child of God."—Vol. vii., p. 82.

"A few met at Mr. Hunter's room, who were athirst for 'full sanctification.'"

"'Entire salvation from inbred sin' can hardly be insisted upon either in preaching or prayer, without a particular blessing."—Vol. vii., p. 181.

"I believe, within five weeks, six in one class have received remission of sins, and five in one band received a 'second blessing.'" "It is exceeding certain that God did give you the 'second blessing,' properly so called. He delivered you from the 'root of bitterness,' from 'inbred' as well as 'actual sin.'" Vol. vii., p. 45. "All agreed," says Tyerman, "that the 'second blessing,' as it was then termed, was to be obtained by simple faith."

This must suffice to show that Mr. Wesley was not confined to any one term in defining his doctrine, but, following the Scriptures, he employed a variety of terms.

Mr. Wesley seems to have had no particular fondness for the term 'perfection,' aside from the fact that it was a Scripture term. His language is "I have no particular fondness for the term 'perfection.' It seldom occurs, either in my preaching or writings. It is my opponents who thrust it upon me continually, and ask what I mean by it. I do not build any doctrine thereupon, nor undertake critically to explain it."

"What is the meaning of perfection? is another question; but that it is a scriptural term, is undeniable, therefore none ought to object to the term, whatever they may as to this or that explication of it." "But I still think that perfection is only another term for holiness, or the image of God in man. 'God made man perfect,' I think is just the same as 'He made him holy,' or 'in his own image.'" —Vol. vi., p. 535.

What, then, are Mr. Wesley's views of Christian perfection or entire sanctification?

1. It is not the" repression" of the evils of the heart, to such an extent as to keep them in subjection, or under proper control.

The theory of "repression," or "subjugation," has been put forth with great vigor. It has been defined as follows:

"Sanctification is such a measure of power over sin as holds the soul with more or less continuity in the same perfect fullness of divine approbation, as rested upon us when justification first pronounced us, through Christ, perfectly innocent of sin."—*Methodist Quarterly Review.*

The plain meaning of this language is: "Sanctification is the continuance, with more or less interruption, of our full, or perfect justification." If a believer retains his justification, with more or less interruption, he is fully sanctified. The language means this and no more.

But this standard of sanctification is clearly below that of uninterrupted justification; for this "full justification," which constitutes entire sanctification, is "with more or less continuity," or interruption. This standard of sanctification is not even equal to uninterrupted justification.

This view of sanctification falls below the Wesleyan standard of justification, as a few facts will show.

At the Conference of 1744, they discussed, and settled the following question:

"What are the immediate fruits of 'justifying' faith?"

"Answer:—Peace, joy, love, 'power over all outward sin, and power to keep down inward sin.'"

In his sermon on "The Marks of the New Birth," Mr. Wesley says: "An immediate and constant fruit of this faith whereby we are born of God, fruit which can in nowise be separated from it, no, not for an hour, is 'power over sin:' 'power over outward sin' of every kind; and power over inward sin."—Vol. i., p. 155.

It seems from this that Mr. Wesley taught a justification more abiding than this new notion of sanctification. His view of sanctification was that it did not simply "repress," sin or subjugate it, but expelled it from the heart. With him it was "entire deliverance from sin," "death to sin," "cleansed from all unrighteousness." Speaking of being cleansed from all sin, he says, "Neither let any sinner against his own soul say that this relates to justification only, or the cleansing us from the 'guilt of sin;' first, because this is confounding together what the apostle clearly distinguishes, who mentions first, to 'forgive us our sins,' and then to 'cleanse us from all' unrighteousness."—Vol. i., p. 367.

The hymns of the Wesleys are full of the idea of cleansing," but nowhere speak of "repression" or subjugation. We cite the following:—

"The original offense,
Out of my soul erase;
Enter thyself, and drive it hence,
And take up all the place."

"Purge me from every sinful blot;
My idols all be cast aside;
Cleanse me from every evil thought,
From all the filth of self and pride."

"Speak the second time, Be clean!
Take away my inbred sin,
Every stumbling-block remove,
Cast it out by perfect love."

"The hatred of my carnal mind,
Out of my flesh at once erase," etc.

"Cast out the foe, the inbred sin,
The carnal mind remove."

These citations must suffice to show that the idea of "repression" found no place in Mr. Wesley's views of entire sanctification. It was "purge," "cleanse," "cast hence," " be clean," "remove," etc.

2. It was the possession of a clean heart, or the mind of Christ.

This perfectly accords with Mr. Wesley's definitions, which run through all his works; as for example: "To be holy is to have a mind that was in Christ, and to walk as he walked." "It is that habitual disposition of the soul which, in the sacred writings, is termed holiness, and which directly implies the being cleansed from all sin, from all filthiness, both of flesh and spirit, and by consequence, the being endued with those virtues which were in Christ."

Mr. Wesley says: "Absolute, or infallible perfection I never contended for. Sinless perfection I do not contend for, seeing it is not scriptural. A perfection such as enables a person to fulfill the whole law, and so needs not the merits of Christ,—I acknowledge no such perfection; I do now and always did, protest against it."—Vol. vi., p. 752.

Not Exemption from Mistakes.

"Certainly sanctification (in the proper sense) is 'an instantaneous deliverance from all sin'; and includes 'an instantaneous power then given, always to cleave to God.' Yet this sanctification (at least, in the lower degrees) does not include a power never to think a useless thought, nor ever speak a useless word. I, myself, believe that such a perfection is inconsistent with living in a corruptible body: for this makes it impossible 'always to think right.' While we breathe, we shall, more or less, mistake. If, therefore, Christian perfection implies this, we must not expect it till after death.

"I want you to be all love. This is the perfection I believe and teach. And this perfection is consistent with a thousand nervous disorders, which that high-strained perfection is not. Indeed, my judgment is, that (in this case particularly) to overdo is to undo; and that to set perfection too high (so high as no man that we ever heard or read of attained) is the most effectual (because unsuspected) way of driving it out of the world."—*Works,* Vol. vi., p. 718.

Deliverance from Inbred Sin.

"It is a second change, whereby we are saved from all sin and perfected in love." "A deliverance from 'inbred' as well as actual sin."

"Christian perfection does not imply an exemption either from ignorance, or mistakes, or infirmities, or temptations. It is only another term for holiness. These are two names for the same thing. Thus, every man that is holy is, in the scriptural sense, perfect."

"Entire sanctification, or Christian perfection, is neither more nor less than pure love; love expelling sin, and governing both the heart and the life of a child of God."

"This doctrine," says Mr. Wesley, "is the grand depositum which God has lodged with the people called Methodists, and for the sake of propagating this chiefly, he appears to have raised us up."

Here is another form of stating the subject.

"But what is the perfection here spoken of? It is not only a deliverance from doubts and fears, but from sin; from all inward, as well as outward sin; from evil desires, and evil tempers, as well as from evil words and works. Yea, and it is not only a negative blessing, a deliverance from all evil dispositions, implied in that expression, 'I will circumcise thy heart'; but a positive one likewise; even the planting all good dispositions in their place; clearly implied in that expression, 'To love the Lord your God with all your heart, and with all your soul.'"—*Sermons,* Vol. ii., p. 410.

Not Impossible to Fall.

"I do not include an impossibility of falling from it, either in part, or in whole. Therefore, I retract several expressions in our hymns, which partly express, partly imply, such an impossibility. And I do not contend for the term 'sinless,' though I do not object against it."

Perfection Scriptural.

"As to the word 'perfection,' it is scriptural; therefore, neither you nor I can in conscience object to it, unless we would send the Holy Ghost to school, and teach Him to speak who made the tongue.

"By Christian perfection, I mean (as I have said again and again) the so loving God and our neighbor as to 'rejoice evermore, pray without ceasing, and in everything give thanks.' He that experiences this is scripturally perfect. And if you do not yet you may experience it; you surely will, if you follow hard after it, for the Scripture cannot be broken."

No Perfection of Degrees.

"There is no 'perfection of degrees,' as it is termed; none which does not admit of a continual increase. So that how much soever any man has attained, or how high a degree soever he is perfect, he hath still need 'to grow in grace,' and daily to advance in the knowledge and love of God his Savior."—*Sermons,* Vol. i., p. 358.

Christian Perfection Reasonable.

"I had once the opportunity of speaking a few minutes to you on the head of Christian perfection; and I believe you had not much objection to anything which was then spoken. When I spoke nearly to the same effect to one of the late bishops of London, Bishop Gibson, he said earnestly, 'Why, Mr. Wesley, if this is what you mean by perfection, who can be against it?' I believe verily, there would need no more than a single hour, spent in free and open conversation, to convince you that none can rationally or scripturally say anything against the perfection I have preached for thirty years."—*Works,* Vol. vi., p. 747.

"Let Christian perfection," says Wesley, "appear in its own shape, and who will fight against it? It must be disguised before it can be opposed. It must be covered with a bear skin first, or even the wild beasts of the people will scarce be induced to worry it."

Love Expelling Sin.

"Entire sanctification, or Christian perfection, is neither more nor less than pure love; love expelling sin, and governing both the heart and life of a child of God."—*Works,* Vol. vii., p. 82.

"Nor did I ever say or mean any more by perfection than 'the loving God with all our heart, and serving him with all our strength'; for it might be attended with worse consequences than you seem to be aware of. If there be a mistake, it is far more dangerous on the one side than on the other. If I set the mark too high, I drive men into needless fears; if you set it too low, you drive them into hell fire."—*Works,* Vol. vi., p. 535.

Sin Not in the Body.

"But surely we cannot be saved from sin, while we dwell in a 'sinful body.' A 'sinful body'? I pray observe, how deeply ambiguous, how equivocal, this expression is! But there is no authority for it in Scripture: the word, 'sinful body,' is never found there. And as it is totally unscriptural, so it is palpably absurd. For no 'body,' or matter of any kind, can be 'sinful;' spirits alone are capable of sin. Pray, in what part of the body should sin lodge? It cannot lodge in the skin, nor in the muscles, or nerves, or veins, or arteries; it cannot be in the bones any more than in the hair or nails. Only the soul can be the seat of sin."— *Sermons,* Vol. ii., p. 172.

Perfection Further Defined.

"I think it was in the latter end of the year 1740, that I had a conversation with Dr. Gibson, then bishop of London, at Whitehall. He asked me what I meant by perfection. I told him without any disguise or reserve. When I ceased speaking, he said, 'Mr. Wesley, if this be all you mean, publish it to all the world. If any one then can confute what you say, he may have free leave.' I answered, 'My lord, I will;' and accordingly wrote and published the sermon on Christian perfection.

"In this I endeavored to show, (1.) In what sense Christians are not, (2.) In what sense they are, perfect.

"(1.) In what sense they are not. They are not perfect in knowledge. They are not free from ignorance, no, nor from mistakes. We are no more to expect any living man to be infallible, than to be omniscient. They are not free from infirmities, such as weakness or slowness of understanding, irregular quickness or heaviness of imagination. Such in another kind are impropriety of language, ungracefulness of pronunciation; to which one might add a thousand nameless defects, either in conversation or behavior. From such infirmities as these none are perfectly freed till their spirits return to God; neither can we expect till then to be wholly freed from temptation; for 'the servant is not above his master.' But neither in this sense is there any absolute perfection on earth. There is no perfection of degrees, none which does not admit of a continual increase.

"(2.) In what sense, then, are they perfect? Observe, we are not now speaking of babes in Christ, but adult Christians. But even babes in Christ are so far perfect as not to commit sin. This St. John affirms expressly; and it cannot be disproved by the examples of the Old Testament. For what if the holiest of the ancient Jews did sometimes commit sin? We cannot infer from hence, that 'all Christians do and must commit sin as long as they live.'"

It has been objected to these views of Christian perfection, that they are involved in his view of conversion or justification. "There is no passage of Scripture which Mr. Wesley uses in describing the state of the sanctified that he does not, somewhere, apply to the state of the regenerated. All he gives to the one he takes from the other, hence, according to Mr. Wesley, regeneration and sanctification are identical."—*Problem of Methodism,* p. 309.

No person, who has read Mr. Wesley carefully, has yet been able to produce one example in which he makes regeneration and entire sanctification identical. And whatever use Mr. Wesley may make of certain texts of Scripture, he never confounds these two doctrines.

A careful examination of Mr. Wesley's teachings on both these subjects will reveal the fact that he does not confound, but keeps the two experiences distinct.

What is Justification?

Mr. Wesley answers: "Justification is another word for pardon. It is the forgiveness of all our sins, and, what is necessarily implied therein, our acceptance with God." "Justification expels the love of the world, the love of pleasure, of ease, of honor, of money; together with pride, anger, self-will and every evil temper." "How naturally do those who experience such a change imagine that all sin is gone, that it is utterly rooted out of the heart, and has no more any place therein. How easily do they draw the conclusion;—I 'feel' no sin, therefore I 'have' none: it does not 'stir,' therefore it does not 'exist': it has no motion, therefore it has no 'being'!" He further says, "Sin remains in him; yea, the seed of all sin, till he is sanctified throughout."

He defines sanctification as "love, joy, peace, always

abiding; but invariably long-suffering, patience, resignation; gentleness, triumphing over all provocation; goodness, mildness, sweetness, tenderness of spirit; fidelity, simplicity, godly sincerity; meekness, calmness, evenness of spirit; temperance, not only in food and sleep, but in all things natural and spiritual."

Mr. Wesley then inquires: "Have we not all this when we are justified?"

"What," he answers, "total resignation to the will of God without any mixture of self-will? gentleness, without any touch of anger, even when provoked? love to God, without the least love to the creature, but in and for God, excluding all pride? love to man, excluding all envy, all jealousy and rash judging? meekness, keeping the whole soul inviolably calm? temperance in all things? Deny that any ever came up to this, if you please, but do not say all who are justified do."

Let those who attempt to convict Mr. Wesley of inconsistency in his descriptions of justification and sanctification, insisting that the one involves the other, carefully mark his distinctions. Mr. Wesley does speak of justification expelling the love of the world, love of pleasure, of ease, etc., but not *all* love of the world, *all* love of pleasure, *all* love of ease, etc. When he speaks of sanctification, it is "love to God without the *'least* love' of the creature;" "love to man, excluding *'all* envy.'" Mr. Wesley believed that all the fruits of the Spirit existed in regeneration, but not in the same measure as in entire holiness. One was the work begun, the other, the work completed. Herein Mr. Wesley is perfectly consistent with himself.

Some have regarded this as a very high state of grace, and have alleged that Mr. Wesley had occasion to modify his views on the subject; and that this modification was rendered necessary by certain troubles known as the "Bell-Maxfield" fanaticism.

It is claimed that Mr. Wesley not only changed his views on the subject, but actually lowered his standard of Christian perfection. One writer says: "Mr. Wesley saw that his 'overstatement of sanctification' had really commenced the (Bell) mischief, and proceeded most wisely to correct his own errors." "He appended to that manual (Plain Account) some very significant notes, carefully and wisely lowering his own overstatement."— *Quarterly Review.*

We think that these assumptions are far from being sustained by the facts in the case.

That Mr. Wesley's mind underwent a slight change on a few minor points is admitted, but that he lowered his standard of entire sanctification, with regard to its nature and properties, is repeatedly denied by him in the most positive terms. Nor can it be shown that the slight changes which did occur, were in any sense influenced by the Bell fanaticism. Let us inquire into the nature of these changes, and the time when they occurred.

At one time Mr. Wesley held that a soul entirely sanctified could not fall. He was convinced of his mistake in this particular, and at once renounced it. Subsequently in speaking of this experience, he says, "I do not include an impossibility of falling from it, either in part or in whole. Therefore I retract several expressions in our hymns, which partly express, partly imply, such an impossibility."— *Works,* Vol. vi., p. 531.

That the Bell trouble did not influence this change, is clear from the following fact: Writing to his brother Charles, in 1767, he says, "Can one who has attained it fall? Formerly I thought not; but you (with Thomas Walsh and John Jones) convinced me of my mistake." Vol. vi., p. 669. Here we find that Thomas Walsh was one of the parties who convinced Mr. Wesley of his mistake. But Thomas Walsh died in 1759, three years before George Bell made any profession of Christian perfection. This fact must put an end to all controversy on that point.

Much is made out of Mr. Wesley's expressions "This is too strong," "This is far too strong," etc. But it will be seen that they have no reference to the "nature and properties" of Christian perfection.

In 1741 Mr. Wesley said that the perfect Christian "desired nothing but the holy and perfect will of God; not supplies in want, nor ease in pain." Of this last expression, he says, "This is too strong, as our Lord himself desired ease in pain." —Vol. vi., p. 492.

At the same time he said that the perfect Christian did not have wandering thoughts in time of prayer. "This," he says, "is far too strong.—See Sermon on Wandering Thoughts."

These are the overstatements of sanctification, of which so much is made. But it must be seen that none of these changes touch the nature of the work of perfect love.

Nor can it be proved that even so slight a change as is here named was the result of the Bell trouble. It is true, they were recorded after that trouble had subsided; and so were the other changes to which we have referred, and which we have proved must have taken place before the death of Mr. Walsh, though no record of the time is made.

Let us see what Mr. Wesley says with regard to changing his views on this subject. He ought to be accepted as good authority.

In a letter addressed to Lady Huntington, as though intended as an answer to these charges, he says, "As to the prophecies of these poor wild men, George Bell and a half dozen more, I am not a jot more accountable for them than Mr. Whitefield is, having never countenanced them from the moment I heard them; 'neither have these extravagancies any foundation in any doctrine which I teach.'" *Tyreman* [*sic*], Vol. ii., P: 463. To show what his doctrine was, and to prove that he never changed his views on the subject, he says: "In one view, it is purity of intention; dedicating all the life to God. It is the giving God all the heart; it is one desire and design ruling all our tempers. It is devoting not a part, but all our soul, body and substance to God. In another view, it is all the mind which was in Christ, enabling us to walk as Christ walked. It is the circumcision of the heart from all filthiness, all inward as well as outward pollution. It is the renewal of the heart in the whole image of God; the full likeness of him that created it. In yet another, it is the loving God with all the heart, and our neighbor as ourselves. Now take it in which of these views you please (for there is no material difference) and this is the whole and soul perfection, as a train of writings prove to a demonstration, which I have believed and taught for these forty years, from the year 1725 to the year 1765."—Vol. vi., p. 530.

The period here fixed extends beyond the Bell trouble, and proves to a demonstration that Mr. Wesley never changed his views on the nature of sanctification.

Sometime after the Bell trouble, reviewing what he had written in 1739, Mr. Wesley says: "These are the very words wherein I largely declared, for the first time, my sentiments of Christian perfection. And is it not easy to see, (1.) That this is the very point at which I aimed all along from the year 1725, and more determinately from the year 1730, when I began to be a man of one book, regarding none, comparatively, but the Bible. Is it not easy to see, (2.) That this is the very same doctrine which I believe and teach to this day; 'not adding one point either to that inward or outward holiness which I maintained eight and thirty years ago'? And it is the same, which, by the grace of God, I have continued to teach from that time till now,"—Vol. vi., p. 488. ·

In 1742 Mr. Wesley published a volume of hymns, in the preface of which, he describes Christian perfection. Speaking of this statement, after the Bell mischief, he says, "This is the doctrine which we preached from the beginning, and which we preach at this day. Indeed, by viewing it in every point of light, and comparing it again and again with the Word of God on the one hand, and the experience of the children of God on the other, we saw farther into the nature and properties of Christian perfection. But still there is no contrariety at all between our first and our last sentiments... We have the same conception of it now, without either addition or diminution."—Vol. vi., p. 495.

These extracts, all written after the Bell trouble, are sufficient to show that there were no such changes in the views of Mr. Wesley, regarding the nature and properties of Christian perfection, as are assumed to have taken place, as the result of the Bell-Maxfield fanaticism. The whole statement is a misrepresentation of Mr. Wesley's views.

Chapter IX.
How May this Experience be Obtained?

Is it gradual or instantaneous?

In the early part of Mr. Wesley's ministry, he does not seem to have been settled upon this point. As he advanced in his work, personal experience threw much light on the subject, and settled in his mind some questions of great value. The question as to whether it was "gradual" or "instantaneous," or "both," was difficult to determine, and not until he was compelled by the testimony of hundreds of his ministers and members, of whose experience he could not doubt, was he forced to regard it as an instantaneous work, preceded and followed, like justification, by a gradual work.

1. Mr. Wesley, at first believed the work was gradual, and to be finally accomplished at or near death.

Speaking of one that is born of God, and only a "babe in Christ," he says, "In the same proportion as he grows in faith, he grows in holiness; he increases in love, lowliness, meekness in every part of the image of God; till it please God after he is thoroughly convinced of inbred sin, of the total corruption of his nature, to take it all away; to purify his heart and cleanse him from all unrighteousness."

This looks very much like a gradual work. It cannot be denied that there are several passages in Mr. Wesley's writings which seem to teach this doctrine. But it must be conceded that as time advanced, and he saw more and more of the work of grace in the entire sanctification of the souls of his members, that he gave up almost entirely the idea of gradual sanctification, and insisted on the "Instantaneous."

The following statement will give the reader some idea of the manner of his coming to this belief:

"I will simply relate what I have seen myself in the course of many years. Four or five and forty years ago, when I had no distinct views of what the apostle meant, by exhorting us to 'leave the principle of the doctrine of Christ, and go on to perfection;' two or three persons in London, whom I knew to be truly sincere, desired to give me an account of their experience. It appeared exceeding strange, being different from any that I had heard before: but exactly similar to the preceding account of entire sanctification. The next year, two or three more persons at Bristol, and two or three in Kingswood, coming to me severally, gave me exactly the same account of their experience. A few years after I desired all those in London, who made the same profession, to come to me all together at the Foundery, that I might be thoroughly satisfied. I desired that man of God, Thomas Walsh, to give us the meeting there. When we met, first one of us, and then the other, asked the most searching questions we could devise. They answered every one without hesitation, and with the utmost simplicity, so that we were fully persuaded they did not deceive themselves."

"In the years 1759, 1760, 1761 and 1762, their numbers multiplied exceedingly, not only in London and

Bristol, but in various parts of Ireland as well as England. Not trusting to the testimony of others, I carefully examined most of these myself; and in London, alone, I found six hundred and fifty-two members of our society who were exceeding clear in their experience, and of whose testimony I could see no reason to doubt. I believe no year has passed since that time, wherein God has not wrought the same work in many others; but sometimes in one part of England or Ireland, sometimes in another;— 'the wind bloweth where it listeth;'—and every one of these (after the most careful inquiry, I have not found one exception either in Great Britain, or Ireland) has declared that his deliverance from sin was 'instantaneous:' that the change was wrought in a moment. Had half of these, or one third, or one in twenty, declared it was 'gradually' wrought in 'them,' I should have believed this, with regard to 'them,' and thought that 'some' were gradually sanctified and some instantaneously. But as I have not found, in so long a space of time, a single person, speaking thus; as all who believe they are sanctified, declare with one voice, that the change was wrought in a moment, I cannot but believe that sanctification is commonly, if not always, an 'instantaneous' work."—*Sermons,* Vol. ii., p. 223.

2. He seems, in the following statement, to settle the question of its instantaneousness: "I have continually testified, for these five and twenty years, in private and public, that we are sanctified as well as justified by faith. And, indeed, the one of these great truths does exceedingly illustrate the other. Exactly as we are justified by faith, so are we sanctified by faith."—Vol. i., p. 338.

The following statement of Mr. Wesley, copied from Hester Ann Rogers' Journal, p. 174, is clear and to the point:

"You may obtain a 'growing' victory 'over' sin from

the moment you are justified. 'But this is not enough.' The 'body of sin,' the 'carnal mind,' must be 'destroyed;' the old man must be slain, or we cannot put on the new man, which is created after God (or which is the image of God) in righteousness and true holiness; and this is 'done in a moment.' 'To talk of this work as being gradual would be nonsense, as much as if we talked of gradual justification.'"

Mr. Wesley explains what he means by "gradual," an explanation which is sometimes overlooked.

"'But does God work this great work in the soul gradually or instantaneously?' Perhaps it may be gradually wrought in some; 'I mean in this sense, they do not advert to the particular moment wherein sin ceases to be.' But it is infinitely desirable, were it the will of God, that it should be done instantaneously; that the Lord should destroy sin 'by the breath of His mouth,' in a moment, in the twinkling of an eye. And so he generally does; a plain fact, of which there is evidence enough to satisfy any unprejudiced person."

It seems that Mr. Wesley's meaning of "gradual" is simply that the "particular moment wherein sin ceases to be," is not discerned by some. And this is a fact well known to experience. But observe how "infinitely desirable" it seems to him, that "sin should be destroyed" "instantaneously" so that the believer can "advert to the particular moment wherein sin ceases to be."

Charles Wesley had doubts at one time on the subject and some persons were quoting him as opposed to his brother. John writes him, in 1767, thus:—

"I still think, to disbelieve all the professors, amounts to a denial of the thing. For if there be no living witness of what we have preached for twenty years, I cannot, dare not, preach it any longer. The whole comes to one point: Is there, or is there not, any instantaneous sanctification between justification and death? I say, yes. You ('often seem' to) say, no. What arguments brought you to think so? Perhaps they may convince me too."—Vol. vi., P: 669.

"If there be no second change, if there be no instantaneous deliverance after justification, if there be nothing but a gradual work of God (that there is a gradual work no one denies), then we must be content, as well as we can, to remain full of sin till death."—Vol. ii., p. 122.

1. "Christian perfection is that love of God and our neighbor which implies deliverance from all sin.

2. That this is received merely by faith.

3. That it is given instantaneously, in one moment.

4. That we are to expect it, not at death, but at every moment; that now is the accepted time, and now is the day of salvation.'"—Vol. vi., p. 500.

Can any one doubt as to the views of Mr. Wesley on the subject of instantaneous sanctification? This was the point he pressed, saying, that "our word does not profit either in regard to justification or sanctification, unless we bring the people to accept it while we speak."

1. "He thought it was to come 'gradually.'" 2. It was "both 'gradual' and 'instantaneous.'" 3. Finally it was, like justification, "given instantaneous, in a moment." And so he exhorts his preachers to "press the instantaneous work," for he had never found a case where the work was not wrought in a moment.

Chapter X.
Heart Purity not Coetaneous with Conversion or the New Birth.

THIS BRINGS US TO a question which has caused more or less discussion in our church. Some persist in asserting that believers are entirely sanctified at the moment they are justified. And more recently it has been urged that Mr. Wesley, in his later years, "cancelled," his lifelong faith of "sin in believers," and accepted this doctrine.

Let us first inquire as to what Mr. Wesley did teach on the subject of "sin in believers;" and secondly, as to whether he ever changed his views.

1. What did Mr. Wesley teach on the subject of "sin in believers?"

The first introduction of this strange doctrine, that there is no sin in him who is born of God, was by Count Zinzendorf, the founder and first bishop of the Moravian church.

Mr. Wesley was, for a time, in loving fellowship with the Count and the Moravian people, but was forced finally to withdraw from them, mainly on account of their unscriptural views on the subject of entire sanctification.

Zinzendorf is represented by Mr. Wesley as saying, "All true believers are not only saved from the 'dominion' of sin, but from the 'being' of 'inward' as well as 'outward' sin, so that it no longer remains in them."

In response to a question propounded by Wesley, in regard to the state of a believer, Zinzendorf says, "The moment he is justified he is wholly sanctified." "Entire sanctification and entire justification being in one and the same instant."

This dogma was strongly and persistently resisted by Wesley, and for the following reasons:

1. Because it was "new," and consequently false. "I do not know," he says, "that ever it was controverted in the primitive church. Indeed, there was no room for disputing concerning it, as all Christians were agreed. And so far as I have ever observed, the whole body of ancient Christians, who have left us anything in writing, declare with one voice that even believers in Christ, till they are 'strong in the Lord, and in the power of his might,' have need to 'wrestle with flesh and blood,' with an evil nature, as well as 'with principalities and powers.'

"And herein our own church (as indeed in most points) exactly copies after the primitive; declares in her ninth article, 'Original sin is the corruption of the nature of every man, whereby every man is in his own nature inclined to evil, so that the flesh lusteth contrary to the Spirit. And this infection of nature doth remain, yea, in them that are regenerated; whereby the lust of the flesh is not subject to the law of God. And although there is no condemnation for them that believe, yet this lust hath of itself the nature of sin.'

"Accordingly, believers are continually exhorted to watch against the flesh, as well as the world and the devil. And to this agrees the constant experience of the children of God. While they feel the witness in themselves, they feel a will not wholly resigned to the will of God. They know they are in Him; and yet find a heart ready to depart from Him, a proneness to evil in many instances, and a backwardness to that which is good."—Vol. i., p.108.

"It has been observed before, that the opposite doctrine, that there is no sin in believers, is quite new in the Church of Christ; that it was never heard of for seventeen hundred years; never till it was discovered by Count Zinzendorf. I do not remember to have seen the least intimation of it, either in any ancient or modern writer; unless, perhaps, in some of the wild, ranting Antinomians. And these likewise say and unsay, acknowledging there is sin 'in their flesh,' although no 'sin in their heart.'"—*Sermons,* Vol. i., p. 111.

Mr. Wesley regarded this as a "new" doctrine, having its origin with Count Zinzendorf, and as such was to be rejected.

2. "He believed that the promulgation of this doctrine was attended with fatal consequences." In 1762, when this doctrine was being pressed by its deluded advocates, Mr. Wesley says, "I retired to Lewisham and wrote the sermon on 'Sin in Believers,' in order to remove a mistake which some were laboring to propagate,—that there is no sin in any that are justified."

Of this doctrine he says, "It tears away the shield of weak believers, deprives them of their faith, and so leaves them exposed to all the assaults of the world, the flesh and the devil."—Vol. i., p. 108.

Again he says, "One argument against this new unscriptural doctrine may be drawn from the dreadful consequences of it. One says, 'I felt anger today.' Must I reply, 'Then you have no faith'? Another says, 'I know what you advise is good, but my will is quite averse to it.' Must I tell him, 'Then you are an unbeliever, under the wrath and curse of God.' What will be the natural consequence of this? Why, if he believes what I say, his soul will not only be grieved and wounded, but perhaps utterly destroyed; inasmuch as he will 'cast away' that 'confidence which hath great recompense of reward;' and having cast away his shield, how shall he 'quench the fiery darts of the wicked one?' How shall he overcome the world, seeing 'this is the victory that overcometh the world, even our faith.' He stands disarmed in the midst of his enemies, open to all their assaults. I cannot, therefore, by any means, receive this assertion, that there is no sin in a believer from the moment he is justified," "because it is attended with the most fatal consequences; not only grieving those whom God hath not grieved, but perhaps dragging them into everlasting perdition." —Vol. i., pp. 110, 111.

"It is true we are then delivered, as was observed before, from the dominion of outward sin; and at the same time, the power of inbred sin is so broken, that we need no longer follow, or be led by it: but it is by no means true, that inward sin is then totally destroyed; that the root of pride, self-will, anger, love of the world, is then taken out of the heart; or that the carnal mind, and the heart bent to backsliding, are entirely extirpated. And to suppose the contrary, is not, as some may think, an innocent, harmless mistake. No, it does immense harm; it entirely blocks up the way to any farther change: for it is manifest, 'They that are whole do not need a physician, but they that are sick.' If, therefore, we think we are quite made whole already, there is no room to seek any farther healing. On this supposition it is absurd to expect a farther deliverance from sin, whether gradual or instantaneous."—*Sermons,* Vol. i., p. 124.

Again, "From what has been said, we may easily learn the mischievousness of that opinion, that we are 'wholly' sanctified when we are justified; that our hearts are then cleansed from all sin." In nearly the same language, he says again, "Hence may appear the extreme mischievousness of that seemingly innocent opinion, that there is no sin in a believer; that all sin is destroyed, root and branch, the moment a man is justified."

By earnestly and constantly preaching on the subject, Mr. Wesley sought to save his people from this delusion. Hence he says:—

"At every place I endeavored to settle the minds of the poor people who had been not a little harassed by a new doctrine which honest Jonathan C—— and his converts had industriously propagated among them,—that 'there is *no sin* in believers; but the moment we believe, sin is destroyed, root and branch.' I trust this plague also is stayed; but how ought those unstable ones to be ashamed who are so easily 'tossed about with every wind of doctrine!'"—*Journal*, June, 1763.

He rejoices that the Methodists of his day were clear and pronounced in their faith on this subject. "It is, then, a great blessing given to his people (the Methodists) that as they do not speak of justification so as to supersede sanctification, so neither do they speak of sanctification so as to supersede justification. They take care to keep each in its own place, laying equal stress on one and the other. They know God has joined these together, and it is not for man to put them asunder; therefore they maintain, with equal zeal and diligence, the doctrine of free, full, present justification, on the one hand, and of entire sanctification, both of heart and life, on the other."—Vol. ii., p. 390.

3. "Wesley rejected this dogma because it was unscriptural."

"I cannot by any means receive this assertion, that there is no sin in a believer from the moment he is justified, because it is contrary to the whole tenor of Scripture."—Vol. i., p. 110.

"There is in every person, even after he is justified, two contrary principles, nature and grace, termed by St. Paul, the flesh and the spirit. Hence, although babes in Christ are sanctified, it is only in part. In a degree, according to the measure of their faith, they are spiritual, yet in a degree they are carnal." This is what Mr. Wesley calls "Sin in Believers."

Some have claimed that Mr. Wesley meant by sin, simply "liability to sinning." But this is far from correct. He used the terms, "infection of nature," "lust of the flesh," "the seed of all sin," "sinful tempers, passions or affections," "pride," "self-will," "lust," "anger," etc. These mean more than "liability," that is, "exposedness." All men, whether holy or unholy, are "liable" to sin; but this is not that "lust," "pride," "anger," "corruption of nature," of which Mr. Wesley speaks in his sermon on "Sin in Believers."

His language is, "And as this position,—there is no sin in a believer, no carnal mind, no bent to backsliding, is thus contrary to the Word of God, so it is to the experience of his children. These continually feel a heart bent on backsliding; a natural tendency to evil; a proneness to depart from God, and cleave to things of earth. They are daily sensible of sin remaining in the heart, pride, self-will, unbelief. Yet at the same time they 'know that they are of God;' they cannot doubt it for a moment. They feel His Spirit clearly 'witnessing with their spirit, that they are the children of God.' They rejoice in God through Christ Jesus, 'by whom they have now received the atonement.' So that they are equally assured that sin is in them, and that 'Christ is in them the hope of glory.' …'That believers are delivered from the 'guilt' and 'power' of sin we allow; that they are delivered from the 'being' of it we deny… Christ, indeed, cannot 'reign' where sin 'reigns'; neither will He 'dwell' where sin is 'allowed.' But He 'is' and 'dwells' in the heart of every believer who is 'fighting against all sin,' although it be not yet 'purified'... Indeed, this grand point, that there are two contrary principles in [unsanctified] believers—'nature' and 'grace' the 'flesh' and the 'spirit'—runs through all the Epistles of St. Paul, yea, through all the Holy Scriptures; almost all the directions and exhortations therein are founded on this supposition, pointing at wrong 'tempers' or 'practices' in those who are, notwithstanding, acknowledged by the inspired writers to be believers."

"What he means by "Sin in Believers" is further described: "By sin, I here understand inward sin: any sinful temper, passion, or affection; such as pride, self-will, love of the world, in any kind or degree; such as lust, anger, peevishness; any disposition contrary to the mind which was in Christ."

Our space will not allow of introducing all Mr. Wesley's words on this point. He argues strongly from the Scriptures, that there is still in those who are born of God, but not fully sanctified.

4. He rejected the dogma that there is no sin in those who are born of God, because it was opposed to experience.

"Only let it be remembered," he says, "that the heart of even a believer is not wholly purified when he is justified. Sin is then overcome, but it is not rooted out; it is conquered, but not destroyed. Experience shows him, first, that the root of sin, self-will, pride and idolatry, remain still in the heart. But, as long as he continues to watch and pray, none of these prevail over him."—Vol. ii., p. 476.

"Your finding sin remaining in you still is no proof that you are not a believer. Sin does remain in one that is justified, though it has not dominion over him. For he has not a clean heart at first, neither are 'all things' as yet 'become new.' But fear not, though you have an evil heart. Yet a little while, and you shall be endued with power from on high, whereby you may 'purify yourselves, even as He is pure;' and be 'holy, as He which hath called you is holy.'"—*Journal,* June, 1740.

Writing to one, he says, "This is not only your experience, but the experience of a thousand believers besides, who yet are sure of God's favor, as of their own existence."—Vol. vii., p. 71.

He says again, "I do not know a single instance, in any place, of a person receiving, in one and the same moment, remission of sins, the abiding witness of the Spirit and a new and clean heart."—Vol. vii., p. 592.

Mr. Wesley found witnesses of this experience in all parts of his work. Here is a clear statement: "In the years 1759, 1760, 1761 and 1762, their number multiplied exceedingly, not only in London and Bristol, but in various parts of Ireland as well as England. Not trusting to the testimony of others, I carefully examined most of these myself, and in London alone I found six hundred and fifty-two members of our society, who were exceedingly clear in their experience, and whose testimony I could see no reason to doubt. I believe no year has passed since that time, when God has not wrought the same work in many others; but sometimes in one part of England or Ireland, and sometimes in another;— as the wind bloweth where it listeth; and every one of these (after the most careful inquiry, I have not found one exception either in Great Britain or Ireland) has declared that this deliverance from sin was 'instantaneous;' that the change was wrought in a moment. And this, be it 'remembered, was a "second" work, an experience coming after justification.

In preaching at Wednesbury, he said, "I can boldly preach the perfection I believe in, because I think I see five hundred witnesses of it."

Speaking of the experience of Susannah Spencer, he says: "From the very time of her justification, she clearly saw the necessity of being wholly sanctified; and found an unspeakable hunger and thirst after the full image of God; and in the year 1772, God answered her desire. The second change was wrought in as strong and distinct a manner as the first had been."—*Journal,* October, 1774.

"Blessed be God, though we set an hundred enthusiasts aside, we are still 'encompassed with a cloud of witnesses,' who have testified, and do testify, in life and in death, that perfection which I have taught these forty years! This perfection cannot be a delusion, unless the Bible be a delusion too; I mean 'loving God with all our heart, and our neighbor as ourselves.' I pin down all its opposers to this definition of it."—*Journal,* August, 1768.

The dogma that there is no sin in those who are born of God, Wesley found to be opposed to the experience of this great cloud of witnesses, and for that reason, among others, he rejected it.

It is claimed that the doctrine of Zinzendorf was simply "imputed" holiness, and that it was this imputation which Mr. Wesley opposed. One writer says: "It must be remembered that the holiness which he (Zinzendorf) described, is 'imputed,' not personal." Others have made the same assertion.

It is true that Zinzendorf taught the doctrine of "imputation;" but he taught the doctrine which is here opposed as well. The two views are clearly stated as follows:

1. "That we are sanctified wholly the moment we are justified."

2. "That a believer is never sanctified or holy in himself, but in Christ only."

Mr. Wesley always kept these two views distinct. He seldom refers to the second dogma, but always antagonizes the first.

In a long conversation with Zinzendorf, when reference was made to the second dogma, Wesley remarked, "We contend, I think, about words." Again, he says, "The dispute is altogether about words." But when Zinzendorf said that "a babe in Christ is as pure in heart as a father in Christ. There is no difference," this was not a "strife about words."

The statements of our modern writers on this dogma are in almost the exact words of Zinzendorf. A writer in the *Quarterly Review,* July, 1878, says, "Every one who is born of God is pure in heart, free from sin and sanctified. And this sanctification is contemporaneous with the new creation. Zinzendorf says, "We are sanctified wholly the moment we are justified; entire sanctification and entire justification being in one and the same instant."

A late advocate of this strange dogma, says: "Every one who is born of God becomes that very hour a 'new creation,' holy, free from sin, cleansed, sanctified, saved."

Zinzendorf says: "The moment he is justified he is wholly sanctified."

These men employ the same terms, and by them mean the same thing. There is no doubt but what this fatal error had its inception in Antinomianism, and entered the church through that dark door, and has crystallized into its present form.

It is not true that Wesley antagonized Zinzendorf's views of "imputed" holiness, but the simple, plain statement that a believer is entirely sanctified when he is born again. And any attempt to evade the issue, and make it appear that Wesley, in his sermon on "Sin in Believers," was antagonizing Zinzendorf's dogma of "imputed holiness," is to array ourselves against all the plain facts in the case.

Did Not Mr. Wesley Change His Views?

It has been falsely assumed by some that Mr. Wesley, late in life, "cancelled" his lifelong views of "Sin in Believers," and adopted the Zinzendorf dogma. This is surely a bold assumption, and demands in its support the clearest and most unquestionable evidence. It is asserted that this remarkable change took place not later than 1784, at, or near the time that Mr. Wesley furnished the "Articles of Religion" for the Methodist Episcopal Church. And the only evidence ever adduced in support of the assumption, that Mr. Wesley abandoned his views on this subject, is that he omitted from our "Seventh Article of Religion," a portion of the "Ninth Article," of the "Thirty-Nine Articles" of the Church of England. This is the important sentence omitted by Mr. Wesley:— "And this infection of nature doth remain in them that are regenerated." This clause omitted is evidence that Mr. Wesley had abandoned his faith in the doctrine of "Sin in Believers," and had embraced the dogma which he had persistently antagonized during his whole ministry, viz., that there is no sin in him that is born of God.

There are several facts which seem to seriously damage this assumption, and go to prove its utter absurdity.

1. For more than forty years Mr. Wesley denounced the dogma that there is no sin in him who is born of God, as a "dangerous doctrine," and "attended with the most fatal consequences," "not only grieving those whom God hath not grieved, but, perhaps, dragging them into everlasting perdition." He calls it a "mischievous doctrine," "a plague," and "contrary to the whole tenor of Scripture."

It would seem that after more than forty years of Scripture investigation, and confirmed faith in this doctrine, he could not have abandoned it in a moment, nor without the most thorough investigation, supported by the most conclusive reasons. It was not a question of minor importance, but one fraught, in his judgment, with far-reaching consequences.

2. If he did abandon the doctrine of "Sin in Believers," he utterly failed to make any direct mention or record of it.

We search the writings of Mr. Wesley in vain to find

an allusion, either in sermon, letter, or counsel to his preachers, to the fact that such a change had occurred. The Wesleyan Body—preachers and people, with few exceptions, it may be, fully accepted Mr. Wesley's views of "Sin in Believers," and is it to be supposed that he had "cancelled" his views, so long and persistently held, without informing them of the change? The assumption is preposterous.

3. If Mr. Wesley abandoned his doctrine of "Sin in Believers," he succeeded in so far concealing the fact, that his most intimate associates and lifelong friends utterly failed to discover it, and his followers, for more than a hundred years, have never had a suspicion of any such change, until Drs. Crane and Boland made the wonderful discovery.

Dr. Adam Clarke, his chief Biblical scholar, Dr. Thomas Coke, his chief missionary, Henry Moore, his honored biographer, Joseph Benson, his fast friend, and others, who were among his confidential admirers, had no knowledge of such a change. It does not seem possible that Mr. Wesley could have made such a fundamental change in what he regarded as the "grand depositum," committed to him and his people, as to have eliminated its chief corner stone, without informing his ministers, especially those whom he had appointed to carry forward and establish his doctrines among men. He who can believe this must be credited with a measure of credulity which is not common to mortals.

Dr. Clarke goes on preaching and writing on the subject, the same as he had done from the beginning.

Mr. Benson and Dr. Coke wrote commentaries, in which they defend the Wesleyan view of "Sin in Believers." Richard Watson, Wesley's ablest and best expositor, does the same thing, following in the footsteps of his illustrious father in the gospel.

Mr. Wesley lived seven years after the "Articles of Religion" were adopted by American Methodism, and yet, in all that time, he observes the most profound silence on the subject of change, and even recommends the circulation of his "Plain Account," as the best exposition of his views, the book which was full of this obnoxious doctrine of "Sin in Believers." Dr. Coke brings these Articles to us containing this remarkable change in Mr. Wesley's views, and not only fails to inform the American brethren of this change, pointing them to the "Seventh Article," from which the "infection theory" is "excluded," but he actually goes on himself preaching the same old doctrine of "Sin in Believers," as if no such change had ever occurred. And Bishop Asbury was so ignorant of this change, that he declared he "preached it in every sermon."

Nine years after Wesley's death, 1800, the British Wesleyan Conference took special action on this subject, showing that the old faith had come down to them, and they were earnestly contending for it. Among other "questions" and "answers" considered by the conference was the following:

"*Question* 17. If any traveling preacher hold the opinion that every justified person is entirely sanctified, when he is justified, what shall be done with such preacher?"

"*Answer.* Any preacher who is proved to hold this doctrine shall engage that while he preaches in connection with the Methodists, he will not preach this doctrine, or propagate it in any meeting or company whatever; and if such traveling preacher be not reclaimed from his error in one year from that time, he shall be suspended from preaching among the Methodists, either as a traveling or local preacher, till he be reclaimed from his error."

Could all this have occurred, had Mr. Wesley renounced his favorite doctrine? He was not a man of "duplicity," as he himself avers. But he must have been such a man to have allowed his ministers and people to be so "misled by his silence on so important a subject. On all doctrinal questions he was transparent; he never withheld his views on any question from the people. And to say that he concealed his views on "Sin in Believers," even by implication or silence, is a reflection upon the good man which should bring the blush of shame to him who declares it.

Mr. Wesley even went so far as to write and publish, some years later, his second sermon on "Christian Perfection," and yet in this sermon he makes no reference to abandoning the doctrine of "Sin in Believers," which he had advocated in his earlier sermon on the same subject. It is claimed that "Mr. Wesley had no time to correct his views on this subject; that he intended to do so, but finally left it to be done by his followers." But here was an opportunity, by a single paragraph, to have given the needed information. He could have said, while writing on that special subject, that he had "cancelled" his views on the doctrine of "Sin in Believers," and that the whole work of renewal was complete at conversion. He does not do it, and for the best of all reasons, no such change had occurred.

4. If Mr. Wesley had "cancelled" his views on the subject of "Sin in Believers," in 1784, how does it appear that he still continued to proclaim the same doctrine to the end of life?

It can be clearly shown that so far from Mr. Wesley having abandoned this doctrine, he continued to preach it as he had done for forty years before.

In 1785, one year after our "Articles of Religion" had been adopted, we find him writing to his preachers and members, pressing the same old doctrine.

Writing to John Ogilvia, in 1785, he says, "As long as you are yourself earnestly aspiring after full deliverance from all sin, and a renewal in the whole image of God, God will prosper you in your labors; especially if you constantly and strongly exhort all believers to expect full sanctification now, by simple faith."—Vol. vii., p. 147.

These are strong words for one who believed that full sanctification is received at conversion.

In the same year, 1785, we find him pressing the same old subject. Writing to Miss Ritchie, of the work in Dublin, he says, "Many are convinced of sin, many justified, and not a few perfected in love."—Vol. vii., p. 183.

Addressing a letter, the same year, to Freeborn Garrettson, giving him directions in regard to young converts, he says: "It is well, as soon as they find peace with God, to exhort them to go on unto perfection! The more explicitly and strongly you press believers to aspire after full sanctification, as attainable now by simple faith, the more the whole work of God will prosper."—Vol. vii., p. 184. Let us not fail to observe that Mr. Wesley employs the terms "perfection" and "full sanctification," as meaning one and the same thing, and both to be received by those who already enjoyed "peace with God." And, further, it is not a mere growth, but a blessing, to be "attained now by simple faith."

During this same year, 1785, one year and more after, it is said, he had "cancelled" his doctrine of "Sin in Believers," writing to Miss Cooke, he says: "You know well that one thing, and one thing only, is needed for you upon earth, to ensure a better portion, to recover the 'favor' and 'image' of God. The former, by His grace, you have recovered; you have tasted of the love of God. See that you do not cast it away. See that you hold fast the beginning of your confidence steadfast unto the end. And how soon may you be made a partaker of sanctification! And not only by a slow and insensible growth in grace, but by the power of the Highest overshadowing you, in a moment, in the twinkling of an eye, so as utterly to abolish sin, and to renew you in his whole image! If you are simple of heart, if you are willing to receive the heavenly gift as a little child, without reasoning, why may you not receive it now? He is nigh that sanctifieth; he is with you; he is knocking at the door of your heart."—Vol. vii., p. 199.

Here is a soul who had been "restored to the favor of God," had "tasted of the love of God," exhorted to "hold it fast," and not "cast it away," but to press on until she was "made a partaker of sanctification," and to look for it, not by a "slow and insensible growth in grace," but "in a moment," "so as utterly to 'abolish' sin," and to be "renewed in the whole image of God."

Had Mr. Wesley "cancelled" his doctrine of "Sin in Believers?" If so, he must have fully returned to his old faith again, or he was guilty of giving false counsel to this soul.

In 1787, two years later, writing to Rev. Mr. Peronnet, he says: "Do not forget, strongly and explicitly, to urge the believers to go on unto perfection. When this is constantly and earnestly done, the word is always clothed with power."—Vol. vii., p. 101.

In 1788, still further on, and nearer the end of life, writing to Mrs. Elizabeth Baker, who was already a Christian, he inquires, "Have you a constant witness of the pardoning love of God? And do you find an abiding love to Him?" In addition to this witness of pardoning love and its abiding, he inquires, "Have you yet been enabled to give him your 'whole' heart? If so, at what time, and in what manner did you receive the blessing?"—Vol. vii., p. 216.

In the following year, 1789, writing to the same person, he inquires: "Do you receive a clear, direct witness that you are saved from 'inbred sin'? At what time? In what manner? And do you find it as clear as it was at first? Do you see an increase?"—Vol. vii., p. 217.

In 1791, writing to Dr. Adam Clarke, he says: "If we can prove that any of our local preachers or leaders, either directly or indirectly, speak against it [perfect love], let him be a local preacher and leader no longer. I doubt whether he should continue in the society. Because he that can speak thus in our congregations cannot be an honest man."—Vol. vii ., p. 206.

Only a few months before his death, Mr. Wesley, writing to Mr. York, says, "Whenever you have opportunity to speak to believers, urge them to go on unto perfection. Spare no pains; and God, our own God, still give you his blessing."—Vol. vii., p.238.

A few days earlier, he writes to Edward Lewby thus: "A man that is not a thorough friend to Christian perfection will easily puzzle others, and thereby weaken, if not destroy, any select society. I doubt this has been the case with you."—Vol. vii., p.253.

It will be observed that Mr. Wesley's method of urging "believers" to go on unto "perfection" and thereby obtain deliverance from "inbred sin," was the same subsequent to 1784, as prior to that time. He employs the same forms of expression in both periods, without the slightest intimation that he had in any way, or to any extent, changed his views on the subject. Are not these facts sufficient to convince any reasonable mind that Wesley retained his views of "Sin in Believers" to the end?

I must call the reader's attention to another fact, going to prove that Mr. Wesley taught the doctrine of "Sin in Believers" down to the end of life. In what are known as "The Large Minutes," revised and enlarged from 1744 to 1789, and reprinted from a copy which bears the date of 1791, the year that Wesley died, and collated with the edition of 1789 we have the following question: "What can be done to revive the work of God when it is decayed?" Among the answers given is the following: "Be more active in dispersing the books, 'particularly' the sermons on 'The Good Steward,' on 'Indwelling Sin' ('Sin in Believers'); on 'the Repentance in Believers' and the 'Scripture way of Salvation.'"—Vol. v., pp. 221, 222. Here is Wesley within a few months of his death, urging that the very sermons, which contain his strongest arguments in defence of the doctrine of "Sin in Believers," be circulated, in order to arouse the people to greater activity. Could this have been done, had Wesley, seven years before, abandoned the doctrine, in support of which, these sermons were mainly written?

On June 11, 1788, while at Yarm, Mr. Wesley wrote his sermon "On the Discoveries of Faith," in which occurs this passage: "To these (young men in experience) more especially we may apply the exhortation of the Apostle Paul: 'Leaving the first principles of the doctrine of Christ' (namely, repentance and faith) 'let us go on unto perfection.' But in what sense are we to leave these principles? Not absolutely; for we are to retain both the one and the other, the knowledge of ourselves, and the knowledge of God, until our lives' end; but only comparatively; not fixing, as we did at first, our whole attention upon them, thinking and talking perpetually of nothing else, but either repentance or faith," [as most professors are doing in these times.] "But what is the perfection here spoken of? It is not only deliverance from doubts and fears, but from sin; from all inward as well as outward sin; from evil desires and evil tempers, as well as from evil words and works. Yea, and it is not only a negative blessing, a deliverance from all evil dispositions implied in the expression, 'I will circumcise thy heart;' but a positive one likewise, even the planting all good dispositions in their place; clearly implied in that other expression, 'To love the Lord with all the heart, and with all the soul.'"—Vol. ii., p. 410.

It will be seen here that Mr. Wesley urges "young men," those who "have overcome the wicked one," to "go on unto perfection," or to a "deliverance from inward as well as outward sin, from evil desires and evil tempers." Does this look as if he had abandoned his doctrine of "Sin in Believers?" And yet this was written six years after he had prepared the "Articles of Religion" for American Methodism.

Two years later, April 21, 1790, while at Halifax, Mr. Wesley writes his sermon on the "Deceitfulness of Man's Heart," in which occurs this passage: "Only let it be remembered that the heart, even of a believer, is not wholly purified when he is justified. Sin is then overcome, but it is not rooted out; it is conquered, but not destroyed. Experience shows him, *first,* that the roots of sin, self-will, pride and idolatry, remain still in the heart. But as long as he continues to watch and pray, none of them shall prevail against him. Experience teaches him, secondly, that sin (generally pride and self-will), cleave to his best actions. So that even with regard to these, he finds an absolute necessity for the blood of atonement."—Vol. ii., p. 476.

Could he have stated his doctrine of "Sin in Believers" more clearly? Did he ever state it differently?

March 26, 1790, being at Madely, the late home of the sainted Fletcher, he says, "I finished my sermon on the *Wedding Garment,* perhaps the last that I shall write. My eyes are now waxed dim, my natural force is abated." In the sermon he inquires, "What is that holiness which is the true wedding garment?" He proceeds to define it as he had done from the beginning: "It first, through the energy of God, worketh love to God and all mankind; and by this love every holy and heavenly temper. In particular, lowliness, meekness, gentleness, temperance and long suffering." "It is keeping the commandments of God, particularly those, 'Thou shalt love the Lord thy God with all thy heart, and thy neighbor as thy self.' In a word, holiness is the having the mind that is in Christ, and the walking as Christ walked." He then goes on to say, "Such has been my judgment for three-score years, without any material alteration. Only about fifty years ago I had a clearer view than before of justification by faith, and in this, from that very hour, I never varied, no, not a hair's breadth. Nevertheless, an ingenious man has publicly accused me of a thousand variations. I pray God not to lay this to their charge. I am now on the borders of the grave, but by the grace of God, I still witness the same confession." Here is a positive denial that he had ever changed his views of justification or holiness "a hair's breadth in fifty years." And this denial is made less than one year before he died, and nine years after it is claimed he had "cancelled" his views on the doctrine of "Sin in Believers."

Still the question returns, What explanation can be given of Mr. Wesley's omission of the "infection of nature" clause from the Seventh Article?

This Article, as it stands in the "Ninth" of the Church of England, and the "Seventh" in the Articles of Religion of the Methodist Church, placed side by side, will give the reader a clear idea of the change made by Mr. Wesley. We give, first the original and then the revised.

"Of the original or birth sin. Original sin standeth not in the following of Adam (as the Pelagians do vainly talk), but it is the fault or corruption of the nature of every man, that naturally is engendered of the offspring of Adam, whereby man is very far gone from original righteousness, and is of his own nature inclined to evil, so that the flesh lusteth always contrary to the spirit, and, therefore, in every person born into the world it deserveth God's wrath and damnation: And this infection of nature doth remain, yea in them that are regenerated, whereby the lust of the flesh, called in the Greek φρονημα σαρκος which some do expound the wisdom, some sensuality, some the affections, some the desire of the flesh, is not subject to the Law of God. And, though there is no con-

demnation for them that believe and are baptized, yet the Apostle doth confess, that concupiscence and lust hath of itself the nature of sin."

Let us now give the Article as it appears in the Articles of Religion of the Methodist Church.

"Original sin standeth not in the following of Adam (as the Pelagians do vainly talk), but it is the corruption of the nature of every man, that naturally is engendered of the offspring of Adam, whereby man is very far gone from original righteousness, and of his own nature inclined to evil, and that continually."

In making changes in the original "Thirty-nine" Articles, Mr. Wesley entirely omitted fifteen, abridged three, and made verbal alterations in some others.

There were several errors in the Ninth Article which Wesley could not accept. He sought to retain the doctrine of "original or birth sin" in its simplest form. The original Article states that "every person born into the world deserveth God's wrath and damnation." This dogma Wesley rejected, believing that no one "deserved God's wrath and damnation" until he had become an actual transgressor.

The Article further states, and in the same sentence, that this corruption, or "infection of nature," which "deserveth God's wrath and damnation," "doth remain, yea, in them that are regenerated." This Wesley denied. He believed and taught that an "infection of nature did remain in them that are regenerated, until they are wholly sanctified," but it was not an "infection" which rendered them "deserving of God's wrath and damnation." He, therefore, to avoid this Calvinistic heresy, omitted it.

There is another error in this Ninth Article which Mr. Wesley rejected, viz., the doctrine of baptismal regeneration, found, in these words: "And though there is no condemnation for them that believe and are 'baptized,'" etc. However Mr. Wesley may have been tinctured with this error in his early ministry, it is certain that he had fully abandoned it, and consequently dropped it out of this Article.

Then, this portion of the Article had been interpreted to the detriment of true piety. While every Christian Church, since Apostolic times, held the doctrine of "Sin in Believers," "some," he says, "seem to carry it too far; so describing the corruption of heart in a believer, as scarcely to allow that he has dominion over it, but rather is in bondage thereto; and by this means they leave hardly any distinction between a believer and an unbeliever." Vol. i., p. 108. To avoid this sad mistake, which is still prevalent, Mr. Wesley wisely omitted this whole section of the Article.

The doctrine that there is no sin in him who is born of God, was found in no church creed since Christianity had its birth. The doctrine that regeneration does not remove all depravity, was universally accepted.

It is true that a few persons, under the leadership of Count Zinzendorf, had taught this dogma. But they had been driven to the wall by Wesley, and had mainly abandoned the error.

Then the theory was so entirely contrary to the experience of God's children, that it was not supposed that any sensible person would ever think of adopting it. Only now and then one in the past was known to have held it, and they were, as Wesley says, "wild, ranting Antinomians;" and such characters he did not look for among Methodists.

We think we have now shown that Wesley held and taught the doctrine of "Sin in Believers;" that he never abandoned this doctrine, but taught it to the end of life.

The simple omission of this doctrine from our "'Articles' [*sic*] of Religion" is no more evidence of its having been abandoned by Wesley than the omission of the doctrine of endless punishment. That is in the original Articles, but was not retained in ours. The same may be said of several other doctrines. For example: Mr. Wesley made the witness of the Spirit a very prominent doctrine in his preaching and writings. But the witness of the Spirit cannot be found in the Articles. Is it therefore "cancelled" in Wesleyan theology?

The sanctity of the Sabbath was urged by Wesley and is firmly believed by Methodism. But it is nowhere found in the Articles. Is it therefore "cancelled?"

Are not the reasons we have given for this omission, more in harmony with sound common sense, than that Mr. Wesley had abandoned his lifelong faith on this subject?

Chapter XI.
Mr. Wesley Taught that the Spirit Witnessed to the Experience of Entire Sanctification.

We need not say that this doctrine has been persistently denied. We shall not attempt to prove the doctrine, but simply present Mr. Wesley's views on the subject. It has been stated that Wesley did not teach the "direct" witness of the spirit to entire sanctification. "He taught *a* witness, but not *the* witness." Let Mr. Wesley speak for himself, and then deny it who can. "None," he says, "ought to believe that the work is done till there is added the testimony of the Spirit witnessing his entire sanctification as clearly as his justification." —*Plain Acc.*, p.79.

Speaking of the witness to justification and sanctification, he says, "In general, the 'latter testimony' of the Spirit is both as 'clear' and as 'steady' as the former."—*P. Acc.*, p. 119.

"Since my last account, many have been sanctified, and several justified. One of the former is William Moor.

He was a long time struggling for the blessing; and one night he was resolved not to go to bed without it. He continued wrestling with God for two hours, when he felt a glorious change, and 'the Spirit of God witnessing that the work was done.'"—*Journal,* May, 1762.

He addresses Miss I. C. M., in 1762, as follows:

"When you were justified, you had a 'direct witness' that your sins were forgiven; afterward this witness was frequently intermitted and yet you did not doubt of it. In like manner 'you have had a direct witness that you are saved from sin,' and this witness is frequently intermitted; and yet even then you do not doubt of it. But I much doubt if God withdraws either the one witness or the other without some occasion given on our part. I never knew any one receive the abiding witness gradually; therefore I incline to think this also is given in a moment."—*Works,* Vol. vii., p. 250.

To Mrs. A. F., 1764:—

"In the 'Thoughts on Perfection,' it is observed that, before any can be assured they are saved from sin, they must not only feel no sin, but 'have a direct witness' of that salvation. And this several have had as clear as S— R—has, who afterwards fell from that salvation; although S— R—, to be consistent with her scheme, must deny they ever had it; yea, and must affirm that witness was either from nature or from the devil. If it was really from God, is He well pleased with this?"—*Works,* Vol. vii., p.15.

To Miss J. C. M., 1764:—

"You are a living witness of two great truths: The one, that there cannot be a lasting, steady enjoyment of pure love 'without the direct testimony of the Spirit concerning it'; without God's Spirit shining on His own work: the other, that setting perfection too high is the ready way to drive it out of the world."—*Works,* Vol. vii., p. 250.

Addressing Rev. John Mason, in 1768, he says, "If

any deny the 'witness of sanctification' and occasion disputing in the select society, let him or her meet therein no more."

Writing to one of his members, he says: "One of our preachers has lately advanced a 'new position among us,'—that there is no 'direct' or immediate witness of sanctification, but only a perception or consciousness that we are changed, filled with love, and cleansed from sin. But if I understand you right, you find a 'direct' testimony."—Vol. vii., p.50.

It seems that to deny the "direct witness" of the Spirit to sanctification, was a "new position" among the Methodists of Wesley's time, and an error grave enough to exclude those who spoke in its defence from the "select societies," or holiness meetings.

Mr. Wesley places the witness of the spirit to our justification, and to our sanctification on the same grounds, and sustains his position by the same scriptural authority.

"How do you know that you are sanctified, saved from your inbred corruption?

"I can know it no otherwise than I know that I am justified. 'Hereby know we that we are of God,' in either sense, 'by the spirit that He hath given us.'"

"But what need is there of it, seeing sanctification is a real change, not a relative only, like justification?

"But is the new birth a relative change only? Is not this a real change? Therefore, if we need no witness of our sanctification, because it is a real change, for the same reason, we should need none, that we are born of, or are the children of God."

Mr. Wesley found this doctrine, not only in the experience of his members, but in the Word of God.

"But what Scripture makes mention of any such thing, or gives any reason to expect it?

"That Scripture, 'We have received, not the spirit that

is of the world, but the Spirit which is of God; that we may know the things which are freely given us of God.' 1 Cor. 2:12.

"Now surely sanctification is one of 'the things which are freely given us of God.' And no possible reason can be assigned why this should be excepted, when the Apostle says, 'We receive the Spirit' for this very end, 'that we may know the things which are thus 'freely given us.'

"Is not the same thing implied in that well-known Scripture, 'The Spirit itself witnesses with our spirit, that we are the children of God'? Rom. 8:16. Does He witness this only to those who are children of God in the lowest sense? Nay, but to those also who are such in the highest sense. And does He not witness, that they are such in the highest sense? What reason have we to doubt it?

"What if a man were to affirm (as, indeed, many do) that this witness belongs only to the highest class of Christians? Would not you answer, 'The Apostle makes no restriction; therefore, doubtless, it belongs to all the children of God'? And will not the same answer hold, if any affirm, that it belongs only to the lowest class?

"Consider likewise 1 John 5:19: 'We know that we are of God.' How? 'By the Spirit that He hath given us.' Nay, 'hereby we know that He abideth in us.' And what ground have we, either from Scripture or reason, to exclude the witness, any more than the fruit, of the Spirit, from being here intended? By this, then, also, 'we know that we are of God,' and in what sense we are so; whether we are babes, young men, or fathers, we know in the same manner.

"Not that I affirm that all young men, or even fathers, have this testimony every moment. There may be intermissions of the direct testimony that they are thus born of God; but these intermissions are fewer and shorter as they grow up in Christ; and some have the testimony both of their justification and sanctification, without any intermission at all; which, I presume, more might have, did they walk humbly and closely with God."

Nothing can be plainer than that Mr. Wesley taught clearly and constantly. the doctrine of the witness of the Spirit to our entire sanctification.

Chapter XII.
Mr. Wesley Believed that the Preaching of Christian Perfection "Strongly, Constantly, Explicitly" Promoted the Whole Work of God.

THE MANNER OF PREACHING this doctrine, viz., "strongly, constantly, explicitly" looks to a bold, vigorous style of pressing the subject: "strongly;" meaning firmly, steadily; "constantly— "continually, perseveringly; "explicitly;" plainly, expressly, without disguising its real meaning—not by inference or mere implication, bringing it in "adroitly," as one preacher said he did, that the people might not know what he was doing. It is to be preached so clearly that the most ignorant may be able to understand it, and easily learn the way to its personal realization.

"Let all our preachers make a point to preach of perfection to believers 'strongly,' 'constantly,' 'explicitly.' I doubt not we are not explicit enough in speaking of full sanctification, either in public or private."—Vol. vi., p. 529.

To a member he writes: "I believe you may speak without reserve to Brother Howard. He is a cool-thinking man. But does he preach Christian perfection clearly and explicitly? Which of your preachers does?"—Vol. vii., p. 43.

In a letter to Mr. Merryweather, in 1766, he says:

"Where Christian perfection is not strongly and explicitly preached, there is seldom any remarkable blessing from God; and, consequently, little addition to the society, and little life in the members of it. Therefore, if Jacob Rowell is grown faint, and says but little about it, do 'you' supply his lack of service. Speak, and spare not. Let not regard for any man induce you to betray the truth of God. Till you press the believers to expect full salvation 'now,' you must not look for any revival."—Vol. vi., p. 761.

Of Cornwall, he says: "The more I converse with the believers in Cornwall, the more I am convinced that they have sustained great loss, for want of hearing the doctrine of Christian perfection clearly and strongly enforced. I see, wherever this is not done, the believers grow dead and cold. Nor can this be prevented, but by keeping up in them an hourly expectation of being perfected in love. I say an hourly expectation; for to expect it at death, or some time hence, is much the same as not expecting it at all."—*Journal*, September, 1762.

Speaking of one of his preachers, he says: "I hope he is not ashamed to preach full salvation, receivable now, by faith. This is the word which God will always bless, and which the devil peculiarly hates; therefore, he is constantly stirring up both his own children, and the weak children of God against it."—*Letter to Mrs. Bennis, 1771.*

To his brother Charles, 1772, he writes: "I find almost all our preachers, in every circuit, have done with Christian perfection. They say they believe it; but they never preach it; or not once in a quarter. What is to be done? Shall we let it drop or make a point of it?"—Vol. vi., p. 673.

Have we not fallen upon like times? Ministers say they believe it, but do not preach it once a quarter.

He urges Rev. Mr. Wolf, one of his preachers to "strongly exhort believers everywhere, to 'go on unto perfection,' otherwise they cannot keep what they have."— Vol. vii., p. 122.

Speaking of "Tiverton," he says: "Here I found the plain reason why the work of God had gained no ground in this circuit all the year. The preachers had given up the Methodist testimony. Either they did not speak of perfection at all (the peculiar doctrine committed to our trust), or they speak of it in general terms, without urging the believers to 'go on unto perfection,' and to expect it every moment. And wherever this is not earnestly done, the work of God does not prosper."—*Journal,* August, 1776.

To one of his members he writes, in 1782: "That point, entire salvation from inbred sin, can hardly ever be insisted upon, either in preaching or prayer, without a particular blessing. Honest Isaac Brown firmly believes this doctrine, that we are to be saved from all sin in this life. But I wish, when opportunity serves, you would encourage him, 1. To preach Christian perfection, constantly, strongly and explicitly: 2. Explicitly to assert and prove, that it may be received now; and 3. (which, indeed, is implied therein), that it is to be received by simple faith."—*Works,* Vol. vii., p. 181.

He urges Rev. Mr. Beardsley, "Exhort all the believers, strongly and explicitly to 'go on unto perfection,' and to expect every blessing God has promised, not to-morrow, but to-day." And again, "Everywhere exhort the believers to expect full salvation now by simple faith."

To Dr. Adam Clarke, he writes in 1786, "You do well insisting upon full and present salvation, whether men will bear or forbear."

In an article in the *Arminian Magazine,* referring to a letter from Rev. Alex. Mather, detailing his experience,

Wesley says: "I earnestly desire that all our preachers would seriously consider the preceding account, and let them not be content never to speak against 'the great salvation,' either in public or private; and never to discourage, either by word or deed, any that think they have attained it. No; but prudently encourage them to hold fast whereunto they have attained, and strongly and explicitly exhort all believers to go on to perfection; yea, to expect full salvation from sin every moment, by mere grace, through simple faith."—*Arminian Magazine,* January, 1780.

Can anyone doubt the urgency with which Mr. Wesley pressed his preachers to proclaim this grand truth? And how can we doubt but what we should witness a great spiritual uplift if all our ministers should preach the doctrine and press the experience as Wesley urges?

Bishop Ninde, speaking of the doctrine of Holiness, at the session of one of our Western Conferences, said, "There never was a time when this flower of Christian doctrine needed to be preached more pointedly and clearly than to-day." And for the best of reasons, it is our peculiar doctrine.

"One part of our work is to stir up all who have believed, to 'go on unto perfection,' and every moment to expect the full salvation which is received by simple faith."—Vol. .vii., p. 36.

"This I always observe: where a work of sanctification breaks out, the whole work of God prospers. Some are convinced of sin, others are justified, and all stirred up to greater earnestness for salvation."—Vol. iv., p. 437.

"When Mr. Brackenbury preached the old Methodist doctrine, one of them said, 'You must not preach such doctrine here. The doctrine of perfection is not calculated for the meridian of Edinburgh.' Waving, then, all other hindrances, is it any wonder that the work of God has not prospered here?—Vol. iv., p. 510.

"Entire salvation from inbred sin can hardly ever be insisted upon, either in preaching or prayer without a particular blessing."—Vol. vii., p. 181, 1782.

"Indeed, his work will flourish in every place where full sanctification is clearly and strongly preached."—Vol. vii., p.172, 1785.

"The more explicitly and strongly you press all believers to aspire after full sanctification, as attainable now by simple faith, the more the whole work of God will prosper."—Vol. vii., p. 79.

These citations must suffice to show what was Mr. Wesley's estimate of preaching entire sanctification, "strongly, constantly, explicitly," in order to the promotion of the work of God. He firmly believed that this could not be neglected without damage to the whole work of God.

Chapter XIII.
Wesley Believed that the Subject of Christian Perfection Should be Made a Specialty.

He was accustomed to preach sermons and courses of sermons on the subject, for the purpose of stirring up a special interest among the people.

In London, Nov. 2, 1761, he says, "At five, I began a course of sermons on Christian perfection." Again, "At five in the morning I began a course of sermons on Christian perfection; if haply that thirst after it might return which was so general a few years ago. Since that time, how deeply have we grieved the Holy Spirit of God," 1767. This, it will be remembered, was after the great falling away, as it is called, the result of the Bell and Maxfield fanaticism. Wesley regretted this fanaticism, but he regretted much more the declension in experimental holiness.

No one can read Wesley's *Journals* without being deeply impressed with the frequency with which he preached on the subject of Christian perfection.

In 1738, he says, "When I returned from Germany, I exhorted all I could to follow after that great salvation, which is through faith in the blood of Christ."

"On Saturday evening [Nov., 1739,], I explained, at Bristol, the nature and extent of Christian perfection."

"At Manchester [April, 1761,], in the evening, I met the believers, and strongly exhorted them to 'go on unto perfection.' To many of them it seemed a new doctrine."

"I preached at seven [July, 1761,], on 'Lord, if Thou wilt, Thou canst make me clean?' [*sic*] And oh, what a flame did God kindle? Many were 'on fire, to be dissolved in love.'"

"A large congregation attended at five in the morning [April, 1764,], and seemed to be just ripe for the exhortation, 'Let us go on unto perfection.'"

"At Grimsby, Wednesday [April 4, 1764,], I explained at large the nature of Christian perfection. Many who had doubted it before were fully satisfied."

Sarah Crosby says, "Mr. Wesley left Leeds yesterday. I never heard him preach better, if so well. In every sermon he set forth Christian perfection in the most beautiful light."

"In the evening, the house at Swinfleet not being able to contain a third of the congregation, I preached on a smooth, green place, sheltered from the wind, on Heb. 7:25. Many rejoiced to hear of being 'saved to the uttermost,' the very thing which their souls longed after."—*Journal,* July, 1770.

"The next evening (at Macclesfield) I preached on Rev. 12:14: 'Without holiness no man shall see the Lord.' I was enabled to make a close application, chiefly to those that expected to be saved by faith. I hope none of them will hereafter dream of going to heaven by any faith which does not produce holiness."—*Journal,* April, 1777.

"Forty years ago, I knew and preached every Christian doctrine which I now preach." —*Journal,* September, 1778.

"About ten, I preached at New Mills, to as simple a people as those at Chapel. Perceiving they had suffered much by not having the doctrine of perfection clearly explained, and strongly pressed upon them, I preached expressly on the head; and spoke to the same effect in meeting the society. The spirits of many greatly revived; and they are now 'going on unto perfection.' I found it needful to press the same thing at Stockport, in the evening."—*Journal,* April, 1782.

"In the evening, I exhorted them all to expect pardon or holiness, 'to-day,' and not 'to-morrow.' Oh, let their love never grow cold!"—*Journal* May 1783.

"Friday 6, being the quarterly day for meeting, the local preachers, between twenty and thirty of them, met at West Street, and opened their hearts to each other. Taking the opportunity of having them all together, at the watch-night, I strongly insisted on St. Paul's advice to Timothy, 'Keep that which is committed to thy trust;' particularly the doctrine of Christian perfection, which God has peculiarly entrusted to the Methodists."—*Journal,* February; 1789. This was five years after it is said he had abandoned his views on the subject!

"At nine I preached in the new chapel, at Tunstal; the most elegant I have seen since I left Bath. My text was, 'Let us go on unto perfection;' and the people seemed to devour the word."—*Journal,* April, 1790. Not a word about changing his views.

"We went to Wigan, for many years proverbially called 'wicked Wigan.' But it is not now what it was. The inhabitants in general, have taken a softer mould. The house, in the evening, was more than filled; and all that could get in, seemed to be greatly affected, while I strongly applied our Lord's words, 'I will: be Thou clean.'"—*Journal,* May, 1790. There is no "cancelling" of his views here.

"If I were convinced that none in England had attained what has been so strongly and clearly preached by such 'a number of preachers, in so many' places, and for so long a time, I should be clearly convinced that we had all mistaken the meaning of those Scriptures."—*Plain Account,* p. 88.

The foregoing instances are only specimens of what runs all through his journals. If we consult the journals of Dr. Adam Clarke, Bramwell, Carvosso, Mrs. Hester Ann Rogers, and Lady Maxwell, where a great number of Mr. Wesley's sermons and texts are noticed, we shall find a large proportion of them are on the subject of full salvation or perfection.

2. What he did himself he urged his preachers to do. He was ever exhorting them to "press the instantaneous work," to "speak and spare not," "until you press believers into the experience of Christian perfection, you need expect no general work of God."

To Joseph Benson he writes, in 1782: "I doubt we are not explicit enough in speaking of full sanctification either in public or private."

He urges Mrs. Crosby to "Encourage Richard Blackwell and Mr. Colly to speak plainly, and to press believers to the constant pursuit and earnest expectation of Christian perfection."

He entreats John King to "Earnestly exhort all the believers to follow after full salvation."

To Mr. Merryweather he writes: "Let not regard for any man induce you to betray the truth of God. Till you press believers to expect full salvation 'now,' you must not look for any revival."

These are given simply as examples of what fills his *Journals* and *Letters.* It seemed to be the one purpose of his ministry. Unless this work was being done, almost everything seemed at a standstill.

3. He desired to have it preached, though it might develop fanatics.

In an "address" to the readers of the famous *Arminian Magazine,* for 1780, of which he was "editor," referring to letters written during the great revival of holiness, he says: "I have still abundant letters in my hands, equal to any that have yet been published. Indeed, there is a peculiar energy of thought and language in many of those which were written in the year 1759, and a few of the following years, suitable to that unusual outpouring of the spirit with which both London and many parts of England and Ireland were favored during that happy period. Haply I cannot but call it, notwithstanding the tares which Satan found, means of saving among the wheat. And I cannot but adopt the prayer of a pious man in Scotland, upon a similar occasion: 'Lord, if it please Thee, work the same work again, without the blemishes; but if that cannot be, though it be with all the blemishes, work the same work.'"

4. He believed that special meetings should be held for the promotion of the work of holiness. We are often told that special meetings, held for the promotion of this work, are un-Methodistic—that all our meetings are for holiness.

It can be clearly shown that Mr. Wesley established special meetings for holiness.

Dr. Abel Stevens says: (History of Methodism, Vol. ii., p 452.) "Mr. Wesley established meetings for penitents and backsliders, and select societies for persons who are especially interested in the subject of Christian perfection."

The account given by Mr. Wesley of these select societies is as follows: "I desired a small number of such as appeared to be in this state, [viz., continually walking in the light of God, and having fellowship with the Father and with the Son Jesus Christ] to spend an hour with me every Sunday morning. My design was, not only to 'direct them how to press after perfection,' but also to have a select company to whom I might unbosom myself on all occasions without reserve; and whom I could propose to their brethren as a pattern of love, of holiness, and of good works."—Vol. v., pp. 184, 185.

It will be observed that one of the chief objects of these "societies" was to enable Wesley to "direct them how to press after perfection."

The "Band Meetings" were composed of justified believers who were pressing after holiness. No persons were admitted to these "Bands" unless they could answer the following questions:

"1. Have you forgiveness of sins?

"2. Have you peace with God, through our Lord Jesus Christ?

"3. Have you the witness of the Spirit with your spirit, that you are a child of God?

"4. Is the love of God shed abroad in your heart?

"5. Has no sin, inward or outward, dominion over you?"

If they could answer these questions in the affirmative, they were admitted to the "Bands" as seekers or possessors of holiness.

They were "to meet once a week"; "to come punctually at the hour appointed;" "to begin exactly at the hour with singing and prayer;" "to speak to each other freely and plainly;" "to end each meeting with prayer suited to the state of each person present."

These were meetings expressly for the entire sanctification of believers—persons who were "forgiven," had "peace with God," "the witness of the Spirit," "the love of God shed abroad in their hearts," with "no sin, inward or outward," having "dominion over them."

Mr. Wesley regarded these as among the most profitable of all his meetings. How often he speaks of persons obtaining the "second blessing," the "fulness of love," "entire sanctification," in the "Bands."

5. Mr. Wesley believed that young converts should be immediately pressed into the experience of perfect love.

Writing to Freeborn Garrettson, in 1785, and speaking of young converts, he says: "Whatever they do, let them do it with their might; and it will be well, as soon as they find peace with God, to exhort them to 'go on unto perfection.' The more explicitly and strongly you press all believers to aspire after full sanctification, as attainable now by simple faith, the more the whole work of God will prosper."—Vol. vii., p. 184.

Again Mr. Wesley said, "I have been lately thinking a good deal on one point, wherein perhaps we preachers have all been wanting. We have not made it a rule, as soon as ever persons are justified, to remind them of going on unto perfection; whereas this is the very time preferable to all others."

It will appear, that such as press the subject of holiness as a specialty are simply doing what Mr. Wesley urged all his preachers to do, and the not doing was to hinder the whole work of God.

Chapter XIV.
Advice to Professors of Holiness.

MR. WESLEY GIVES SOME important advice to such as are walking in the light of Christian perfection, which cannot be disregarded. And although it is no part of the "doctrine" proper, it is so connected with the experience, that we think it wise to insert the substance of it here.

1. "Watch and pray continually against pride. If God has cast it out, see that it enters no more; it is full as dangerous as desire. And you may slide back into it unawares; especially if you think there is no danger of it."

"Do not say to any, who would advise you or reprove you, 'You are blind; you cannot teach me;' but calmly weigh the thing before God."

2. Beware of that daughter of pride, enthusiasm. [Fanaticism is the word now.] Oh, keep at the utmost distance from it. Give no place to heated imagination. Do not hastily ascribe things to God. Do not easily suppose dreams, voices, impressions, visions, or revelations to be from God. They may be from Him. They may be from nature. They may be from the devil. Therefore, believe not every spirit, but try the spirits, whether they be of

God. Try all things by the written word, and let all bow down before it. You are in danger of enthusiasm every hour if you depart ever so little from the Scriptures; yea, from the plain, literal meaning of any text, taken in connection with the context."

"Some have left off searching the Scriptures. They say, 'God writes all the Scriptures in my heart, therefore I have no need to read it.' Oh, take warning! Fly back to Christ and keep in the good old way! I say again, beware of enthusiasm. Settle it in your heart, that from the moment God has saved you from all sin, you are to aim at nothing more, but more of that love described in the thirteenth of Corinthians. You can go no higher than this till you are carried into Abraham's bosom."

3. "Beware of Antinomianism; 'making void the law,' or any part of it, 'through faith.' Enthusiasm naturally leads to this; indeed, they can scarcely be separated." "Even that great truth, that 'Christ is the end of the law,' may betray us into it, if we do not consider that he has adopted every point of the moral law, and grafted it into the law of love. Beware of thinking, 'Because I am filled with love, I need not have so much holiness. Because I pray always, therefore I need no set time for private prayer. Because I watch always, therefore I need no particular self-examination."

4. "Beware of 'bigotry.' Let not your love or beneficence be confined to Methodists, so called, only; much less to that very small part of them who seem to be renewed in love; or to those who believe yours and their report. Oh, make not this your Shibboleth!" "Beware of self-indulgence." "Beware of censoriousness." "Thinking or calling them, that any way oppose us, whether in judgment or practice, blind, deaf, dead, fallen, or 'enemies to the work.'"

5. "Beware of sins of omission; lose no opportunity of

doing good in any kind. Do all the good you possibly can to the bodies and souls of men. Be active. Be always employed. Keep at the utmost distance from pious chit-chat, from religious gossiping."

6. "Beware of desiring anything but God. Let them see that you make no account of any pleasure which does not bring you nearer to God."

7. "Beware of schism, or making a rent in the Church of God. Beware of a dividing spirit. Beware of impatience or contradiction. Do not condemn or think hardly of those who cannot see just as we see, or who judge it their duty to contradict what we affirm. All this tends to division.

"Beware of touchiness, of testiness, not bearing to be spoken to; starting at the least word.

"Expect contradiction and opposition, together with crosses of various kinds."

8. "Be exemplary in all things." "In dress." "Avoid every needless expense." "In laying out your money," etc.

We have here presented, in an abridged form, Mr. Wesley's advice to professors of holiness. They are worthy of the most serious consideration. We would do well to humbly consider them, and constantly seek to be governed by them.

Conclusion.

We have done what we proposed. We have presented Mr. Wesley's views of the doctrine of Christian perfection.

In this classification we have seen:

1. That the holiness which he believed in comes after justification, and that he held this view of the subject to the end of life.

2. We have seen also that this experience may be received instantaneously. There is a growth preceding and following the work, in the same sense that growth

precedes and follows the new birth. But both blessings come instantaneously.

3. The experience, in every case, we have found to be by simple faith. Works, properly so called, are entirely excluded, and "exactly as we are justified by faith, so are we sanctified by faith."

4. A clear and humble confession of the experience, in order to retain it, we have found to be the teachings of Wesley. The guards which he throws around the confession of this grace are wise and should be heeded, but the grace must be confessed.

5. That the spirit directly witnesses to this experience. That every argument against this doctrine lies with equal force against the witness of the spirit to our heirship.

6. That special efforts should be made to promote the experience of heart purity. It should be preached, "strongly, constantly, explicitly," and believers should be urged to its immediate reception.

7. That no man can be honest and remain in the Methodist Church, and speak against Christian perfection.

"This doctrine," said Dr. John McClintock, "is our mission." "If Methodism retain this doctrine and experience, the next generation is ours." This doctrine, says the "historian" of Methodism, is "the great potential idea of Methodism."

"If Methodists give up the doctrine of entire sanctification, or suffer it to become a dead letter, we are a fallen people." "Holiness is the main cord that binds us together. Relax this and you loosen the whole system."—*Episcopal Address, 1824*

www.ingramcontent.com/pod-product-compliance
Lightning Source LLC
LaVergne TN
LVHW012340100826
845148LV00018B/3080